THE
COMPASSIONATE
GOD

THE COMPASSIONATE GOD

The Book of Hebrews

Samson Adedokun

© 2010 by Samson Adedokun. All rights reserved.

Pleasant Word (a division of WinePress Publishing, PO Box 428, Enumclaw, WA 98022) functions only as book publisher. As such, the ultimate design, content, editorial accuracy, and views expressed or implied in this work are those of the author.

No part of this publication may be reproduced, stored in a retrieval system, or transmitted in any way by any means—electronic, mechanical, photocopy, recording, or otherwise—without the prior permission of the copyright holder, except as provided by USA copyright law.

Unless otherwise noted, all Scriptures are taken from the *Holy Bible, New International Version®, NIV®*. Copyright © 1973, 1978, 1984 by Biblica, Inc.™ Used by permission of Zondervan. All rights reserved worldwide. WWW.ZONDERVAN.COM

Scripture references marked KJV are taken from the *King James Version* of the Bible.

Scripture references marked NASB are taken from the *New American Standard Bible*, © 1960, 1963, 1968, 1971, 1972, 1973, 1975, 1977 by The Lockman Foundation. Used by permission.

Hard Cover:
ISBN 13: 978-1-4141-1642-6
ISBN 10: 1-4141-1642-X

Soft Cover:
ISBN 13: 978-1-4141-1636-5
ISBN 10: 1-4141-1636-5

Library of Congress Catalog Card Number: 2010906619

DEDICATION

I dedicate this book to my wife, Becky. When we first met, I knew it was my time for blessing. I value your companionship, your love and your kindness. Thank you for making us a family that reflects the goodness of our Father who is in heaven.

To Gamaliel (my first son), who is now deceased, and to IniOluwa, IpinOluwa, and IsuraOluwa, whose support and love I treasure.

To all my friends and fellow workers in His vineyard whom I serve and whose courage and determination remain the sources of my inspiration.

To my father, Ezekiel, and my mother, Esther Abemu, who are now deceased. Without you both, I would not be on this earth. I love you very much.

CONTENTS

Acknowledgments............................... xi

Introduction xiii
    Authorship................................. xiv
    Original Audience............................ xv
    Date xvi
    Theme................................... xvii
    Location of Writer.......................... xvii

Hebrews I: The Supremacy of Jesus Christ........... 1

Hebrews II: Do Not Ignore the Son's Message 9
    A Warning to Pay Attention (2:1-4)................ 9
    The Temporary Abasement of the Son (2:5-9) 11
    The Son's Solidarity with Humanity (2:10-18) 14

Hebrews III: The Superior Faithfulness of The Son ... 19
The Son, as Faithful High Priest, Calls to Faith (3:1-4) .. 19
The Analogy of the Builder (3:5-6) 21
The Faithlessness of Israel in the Wilderness (3:7-19) ... 22

Hebrews IV: The Promise of Final Rest............. 25
Special Diligence Is Needed to Enter God's Rest (4:1-5) .. 26
A Call to Labor to Enter into Final Rest (4:6-11)....... 27
Do Not Reject The Word of God (4:12-13) 29
*Major Appeal: Hold Your Confession and Draw
  Near to God (4:14-16)*...................... 31

Hebrews V: Christ Qualified to Be Compassionate High Priest................................ 35
Requirements for Office (5:1-4).................... 35
The New High Priest (5:5-6)...................... 37
Jesus' Authority to Function as Royal Son (5:7-10) 37
A Call to Spiritual Maturity (5:11-14).............. 39

Hebrews VI: A Strong Warning................... 41
Progressing to Perfection (6:1-3)................... 41
A Warning Against Rejecting the Son (6:4-8) 42
A Word of Encouragement (6:9-12)................. 44
The Certainty of God's Promises (6:13-20)........... 44

Hebrews VII: The Superiority of Melchizedek as High Priest................................ 49
The Meeting (7:1-3) 49
The Meaning of the Two Actions (7:4-10)............ 51
A New Priestly Order (7:11-14) 52
A Priest Forever (7:15-19) 53
The Lord Has Sworn (7:20-22).................... 54
An Eternally Effective Priest (7:23-25).............. 55
A Sinless Priest (7:26-28)........................ 56

Hebrews VIII: The Perfect Sacrifice of the Heavenly High Priest 59

Christ as Minister of a Heavenly Sanctuary (8:1-6) 59
The Inauguration of a New Covenant (8:7-13) 61

Hebrews IX: The Earthly Sanctuary's Appointments . . 63

The Tabernacle (9:1-5) 63
The Priestly Ritual (9:6-10) 64
Eternal Redemption Secured by Blood (9:11-14) 66
A New Covenant Inaugurated in Blood (9:15-22) 67
A Completely Effective Sacrifice (9:23-28) 69

Hebrews X: The Sacrifices Under the Law Were Ineffective 71

The Law Is a Pale Reflection of God's Will (10:1-4) 71
Christ Has Effectively Obeyed God's Will (10:5-10) 72
Christ's Exaltation Shows the Finality of
 His Sacrifice (10:11-14) 74
The New Covenant Brings Effective
 Forgiveness (10:15-18) 77
Hold Your Confession and Draw Near to God (10:19-25) . 78
Do Not Spurn Christ's Sacrifice (10:26-31) 82
Endurance Will Gain the Promised Reward (10:32-39) . . 85

Hebrews XI: The Faith of the Patriarchs 89

The Faith of Abraham and the Early Patriarchs (11:1-22) . . 89
The Faith of Moses and the Exodus Generation (11:23-31) . . 94
The Faith of Subsequent Generations (11:32-40) 96

Hebrews XII: Run With Discipline the Course Set by Jesus 99

God Disciplines His Children (12:1-12) 99
Remove All That Hinders Progress (12:12-17) 102

    Share in the New, Heavenly Worship (12:18-24) 104
    *Final Warning: Do Not Reject God's
        Warnings (12:25-29)* 106

Hebrews XIII: The Offering of Brotherly Love 109
    *Virtues to Be Exhibited in the Persecuted
        Community (13:1-6)* 109
    Life Within the Worshiping Community (13:7-19) 111
    A Personal Conclusion (13:20-25) 114

Bibliography 119

ACKNOWLEDGMENTS

FOR MORE THAN 10 years I have been praying through the power of the Holy Spirit, asking Him to help me to publish my book so that I may offer you encouragement, hope and inspiration. Many people today seem to be dealing with extra burdens brought on by economic hardship even as they face usual challenges to their families, careers, relationships and health. I have struggled with similar circumstances as well, but as long as you have faith in the Holy God, you are not alone.

I was not alone in putting this book together. As usual, I had guidance from the Almighty God, followed by the dynamic publishing professionals at WinePress Group—particularly Athena Dean, Abigail, Jan, Larry, Kevin Cochran and Malcolm. I would like to acknowledge my editor, Simon Presland; the countless hours you spent working on this project will always be appreciated.

I also want to thank my incredible project manager, Adam Cothes, and the entire team at WinePress Group. I thank each of you for humbly submitting to the direction of God for the completion and success of this project. I appreciate all of your contributions.

Special thanks as well to my good friend, Gus Wright, Jr., who found time to read through the manuscript.

INTRODUCTION

INTERPRETING HEBREWS PRESENTS many challenges. We are reading part of a dialogue without any communication from the other party to help us position the letter. Interpreting the letter requires a careful search for clues to anchor the document in historical and social reality and a sensitive ear for hints at an agenda that was perfectly clear to the recipients, if not to us.

The writer assumes that his audience holds common traditions, reads the Old Testament as he does, and shares a view of reality and a store of symbols with which to express it. He assumes that his readers know when he is standing on common ground and when he is moving into new territory. He expects them to follow the logic of his rhetoric so that they will not lose the subtle nuances in his argument.

The author wrote the letter of Hebrews to challenge a community that he saw as being in a perilous situation. He urges them to remain faithful to their confession (3:1; 4:14; 10:23) and warns them not to drift away and neglect their salvation (2:1,3), lose confidence in God's promises

(3:6), fall away from God (3:12), or be rebellious and unbelieving like Israel in the past (3:16-19). His hearers have not progressed to Christian adulthood (5:11-6:2). Having experienced God's saving gift in Christ, they may finally reject Him (6:4-6; 10:29; 12:25). He suggests that their sluggishness (6:12) could lead to something worse—apostasy (10:26). Why the readers are regressing is not clear. The author also hints at a persecution they once endured with joy and concern for others.

The writer's tactics are not merely to appeal for renewed commitment; all of his appeals are based on gospel affirmations. The recipients are to set their sights on Jesus Christ, who is the ultimate revelation of God. As faithful Son and High Priest, He has opened up access into God's holy presence so that those sanctified by Him can offer up sacrifices that are pleasing to God. Neglect of worship is symptomatic of external pressure and inner fatigue, which helps to explain why the letter was meant to be read in worship (13:24-25) and is full of cultic language taken from Old Testament texts that played a role in community worship.

Hebrews asserts the certainty of faith in the context of the Christian cults, viewed primarily as the cultic enactment of divine blessing.

Authorship

"The Epistle of Paul the Apostle to the Hebrews," the title given in the *King James Version*, is not part of the original text of Hebrews but is a later ecclesiastical addition. This early tradition of Pauline authorship was made on shaky foundations; the internal evidence renders such a position untenable:

INTRODUCTION

- Paul insists on his authority as an eyewitness of the risen Lord; the author of Hebrews claims to be a recipient of apostolic witness.
- While Paul can write the smooth prose that is typical of Hebrews, his normal style is argumentative and anacolutha.
- Though Hebrews uses the athletic image that is common in Paul's letters, it has its own distinctive imagery.
- Central theological concepts and themes are markedly different. The explication of the person and work of Christ by analogy with the Old Testament cults and its sacrificial ritual is not common with Paul.

Tertulian (160–200) said the letter was written by Barnabas, but the only support he offers is that Barnabas was a Levite and an encourager. Martin Luther (1483–1546) said it was written by Apollo, because he was eloquent and had a command of the Old Testament. Adolf Harnack (1851–1930) thought that Priscilla wrote the letter and that it had remained unaccredited to hide its possibly controversial female authorship; however, the masculine grammar in 11:32 argues against this.

Original Audience

The author wrote the letter to Jewish Christians, and the thrust of the book seems to suggest they are readers of Jewish background. The phrase at the end of Hebrews, "those from Italy send you their greetings" (13:24), may indicate the author is writing from Italy or that the addressee is a community in Rome who were friends with the author. The second is the more likely interpretation because it has both external and internal support:

1. A Roman document, *I Clement*, is the first to attest of the existence of Hebrews.
2. The term used to describe the "leaders" of the community appears in other early Christian documents connected with Rome.
3. Hints at the support given to other saints by the book's audience were echoed in later tributes that also acknowledge the generosity of Roman Christians.
4. The book of Romans attests to the existence of a number of house churches in Rome. Hebrews could have been directed to one of those churches with whom the writer had a special relationship.

Date

The debate on when the letter of Hebrews was written has focused on two events: (1) the destruction of the Temple in 70 CE, and (2) the Neronian persecution in 64 CE. Use of the present tense to describe the Old Testament cults does not prove that the Temple of Jerusalem was still standing at the time the letter was written. Josephus, writing many years later, also describes aspects of the Temple's appointments and ritual in the present tense. There is a reason, however, to believe that the author of Hebrews wrote it before 70 CE, because if he had written it later, he would surely not have ignored the actual destruction of the Temple as proof that the old cult and its sacrificial system were obsolete. Thus, if we are right in placing the recipient in Rome, the letter must have been written before 64 CE, when Christians began to die for the faith.

INTRODUCTION

Theme

The object of the author's exegesis of the Old Testament Scripture was to give intensity and evidence to the epistle's general theme—the supremacy of Jesus Christ—and to substantiate the finality of the gospel. Jesus Christ possesses all the qualifications needed to be the people's perfect High Priest, for He is personally holy, guileless and undefiled. He could sympathize with these early Christians—and us!—in that He was tempted in all points as they were. This is an exhortation for Christians to remain steadfast in their faith; the complete superiority of who Jesus Christ is and what He has done for them is their sure foundation.

Location of Writer

Tradition is silent as to the place from which the letter was written. There is nothing in the epistle itself that leads to a definite conclusion. Hebrews 13:23 mentions the release of Timothy, but no argument as to the author's location can be made from this because we know nothing about the event to which he was referring. Likewise, the phrase "those from Italy send you their greetings" (13:24) has led some to suppose that the writer was speaking of a small group of friends from Italy who were with him at that time, but so far, the words seem to favor a location of writing in Asia, Syria or Egypt. In any case, it is impossible to lay stress upon a clause, which evidently had a particular and special sense for those to whom the message was sent.

HEBREWS 1

THE SUPREMACY OF JESUS CHRIST

God, who at sundry times and in divers manners spake in time past unto the fathers by the prophets, hath in this last days spoken unto us by his Son, whom he hath appointed heir of all things, by whom also he made the worlds; who being the brightness of his glory, and the express image of his person, and upholding all things by word of his power, when he had by himself purged our sins, sat down on the right hand of the Majesty on high; being made so much better than the angels, as he hath by inheritance obtained a more excellent name than they. For unto which of the angels said he at any time, Thou art my Son, this day have I begotten thee? And again, I will be to him a Father, and he shall be to me a Son?
—Hebrews 1:1-5

THROUGHOUT THE PAGES of Hebrews, the author speaks of the "better things" of Christ. The old covenant was glorious and powerful, but the new covenant in Christ is even more glorious and powerful. The old was a shadow of the new, and the substance of things hoped for. The glories of Israel and the Law with its sacrifices, its priesthood and its ceremonies were only a prelude to that which was to come.

In every action of the old covenant, we see the works of Christ. His life, His death and His resurrection were all in accordance with Old Testament Scriptures and in fulfillment of Old Testament types and prophecies. These prophecies had been given hundreds of years before the coming of Christ through various Spirit-anointed and chosen men. The writer of Hebrews lifts these individuals from the Scriptures.

The lordship of Jesus Christ and His supremacy has always been preeminent in heaven, but He wanted men to recognize His lordship as well. The Gospel of Luke states that before Jesus' birth:

> When Elisabeth heard the salutation of Mary, the babe leaped in her womb; and Elisabeth was filled with the Holy Ghost: And she spake out with a loud voice, and said, Blessed art thou among women, and blessed is the fruit of thy womb. And whence is this to me that the mother of my Lord should come to me?
> —Luke 1:41-43

The lordship of Christ was also the heart and center of the message delivered by Peter on the Day of Pentecost.

The preceding verses bring us face to face with this startling fact: God has taken the initiative in the divine revelation. The opening statement of Hebrews consists of two parallel lines, the first of which is marked by alliteration. God previously spoke in plural ways: to the patriarchs through the prophets. This is an astounding statement! It was necessary for God to speak, for sin had created a barrier between God and man. The opening framing statements outline the superiority of the Son over other agents of

THE SUPREMACY OF JESUS CHRIST

revelation (angels and prophets). Further framing statements picture the royal status of the Son with allusions to the letter's key psalms:

> Ask of me, and I shall give thee the heathen for thine inheritance, and the uttermost parts of the earth for thy possession.
> —Psalm 2:8

> The LORD said unto my Lord, Sit thou at my right hand, until I make thine enemies thy footstool
> —Psalm 110:1

These core statements speak of the divine Son as the wisdom-agent of creation, including the brief reference to "purification for sins." The four central statements picture Christ as royal Son, Divine, Wisdom and royal Priest.

The Hebrew believers had believed the gospel and had experienced its power to change lives. They had tasted of the graciousness of God and the power of the Holy Spirit. Yet they were hesitant; they wavered between Judaism and Christianity. In Hebrews 1:2, the writer begins with an elaborate contrast. Even though he connects past and present revelation, he is not stating that past revelation was defective. It was the penultimate, not the ultimate, word from God. He also states that there is continuity between the ancestors and his audience. The former are the patriarchs and all those in Israel's history who received the word of promise and held to it by faith (see Hebrews 11).

The phrase "last days" recalls the prophetic vision of God's decisive intervention in Israel's history between two ages of redemptive history: the Jewish age and the early Christian age as proclaimed in the books of Isaiah and Jeremiah.

And it shall come to pass in the last days, that the mountain of the LORD's house shall be established in the top of the mountains, and shall be exalted above the hills; and all nations shall flow unto it.
—Isaiah 2:2

The anger of the LORD shall not return, until he have executed, and till he have performed the thoughts of his heart: in the latter days ye shall consider it perfectly
—Jeremiah 23:20

But it shall come to pass in the latter days, that I will bring again the captivity of E'lam, saith the LORD.
—Jeremiah 49:39

The contrast between God's communications to people "in many and various ways by the prophets" and revelation "by a Son" is more striking by the brevity of the second phrase. Revelation through the prophets was promissory in character; it was incomplete, not faulty. By contrast, God's ultimate word through the Son is unique and final. The contrast is between the many and the One (see Hebrews 7:23-24).

The Old Testament speaks of many sons/children of God: Israel ("And thou shall say unto Pharaoh, Thus saith the LORD, Israel is my son, even my firstborn"; Exodus 4:22), angels ("The sons of God saw the daughters of men that they were fair; and they took them wives of all which they chose"; Genesis 6:2), and the king ("I will declare the decree: the LORD hath said unto me, Thou art my son; this day have I begotten thee"; Psalm 2:7). However, in this passage, the author's phrase "a Son" does not imply that He is one among many children (see 2:10-14). The absence of a definite article draws attention to the generic difference

THE SUPREMACY OF JESUS CHRIST

between a Son and any other agent of revelation, especially angels (see 2:2).

Structural analysis of verse 4 forms a closing bracket, with elements running parallel to verses 1-2a. The purpose of verse 4 is not to denigrate the angels; rather, the rhetorical function of the comparison is to extol the Son. The author of Hebrews is simply affirming the Hebrew tradition, reminding his readers that the acquisition of a new name places Christ above the angels. The inheritance of the "name" marks the completion of His messianic mission. The revelation of God's holy name is proclaimed so that Israel could call on it in worship, prayer and praise. The core statements describe the Son as the creative word, identified with the preexistent Wisdom.

Changing the metaphor, the Son bears the stamp of God's own divine being, just as the imprint on a seal or coin corresponds exactly to the die from which it is cast:

> And again, when he bringeth in the firstbegotten into the world, he saith, And let all the angels of God worship him. And of the angels he saith, Who maketh his angels spirits, and his ministers a flame of fire. But unto the Son he saith, Thy throne, O God, is for ever and ever: a scepter of righteousness is the scepter of thy kingdom. Thou hast loved righteousness, and hated iniquity; therefore God, even thy God, hath anointed thee with the oil of gladness above thy fellows. And, Thou, Lord, in the beginning hast laid the foundation of the earth; and the heavens are the works of thine hands: They shall perish; but thou remainest; and they all shall wax old as doth a garment; and as a vesture shalt thou fold them up, and they shall be changed: but thou art the same, and thy years shall not fail. But to which of the angels said he at any time, Sit on my right hand, until I make thine enemies thy footstool?

Are they not all ministering spirits, sent forth to minister for them who shall be heirs of salvation?
—Hebrews 1:6-14

Hebrews 1:6-7 states the divinely ordained function of angels. Here, we see that the angels serve and the Son rules. In the original text, angels are summoned to worship God; here they are to worship the "firstborn" Son, who can be addressed as both God and Lord.

Hebrews 1:7-8 addresses the Son's status. The author is interested in the application to the messianic King in the "today" of his exaltation. God has never addressed an angel as "my Son." This messianic exultation lies behind the acclamation of Jesus at His baptism and His transfiguration. In Hebrews, the author links it with the heavenly enthronement of the Son as God's public proclamation that the King has completed His mission. The enthronement setting established by the inclusion of verses 5 and 13 must apply also to verse 6. Given the enthronement setting, the "world" that the Son enters must be the heavenly realms or the "coming world" of the messianic age, which are inaugurated by His exaltation. Verse 14 further describes the angels' function, paving the way for a final contrast between their limited service and the eternal rule of the Son. Despite their exalted position, angels are merely servants, messengers sent forth to do God's will.

Hebrews 1:9-10 provides God's testimony to this unchanging rule. The text probably came to the writer's mind because he had already cited the prophecy from Nathan in verse 5. What was never true of human kings is fully true of the King who shares God's deity. His rule shares features of God's own reign: righteousness and justice. Oil is the symbol of the richness and prosperity that prevails throughout His rule. The companions of the king are rulers

THE SUPREMACY OF JESUS CHRIST

of other nations; here, the angels are the Son's companions. Like Him, they do God's will, though they are not the Anointed King.

The final text of the chapter (verses 11-14) represents the prayer of an afflicted saint who cries for help. He contrasts the brevity and transitory nature of human existence with the abiding and eternal nature of God. The image of the footstool (verse 13) underlines the absolute sovereignty of the Son. The subjugation of the King's enemies under His feet implies that all—including angels—are His subjects.

The author's final rhetorical question in verse 14 picks up the description of angels as "spirits" and "servants" (he now calls them "serving spirits"). Christ is Himself the "minister" who presides over a new "ministry" that replaces the ritual and legalistic type of worship under the old covenant. The angels have only a subordinate ministry. Because their mission is to serve those who are heirs of salvation, they are lower than humans, but also collaborators with them in worship. The exaltation of the Son is a promise of the believer's own glorification.

God's message is thus spoken in one simple word: Jesus. If we know who Jesus is, we know all that we will ever need. He is the Guide and Shepherd of our lives, and God will speak direction to our path through the Holy Spirit. Today, God's voice is one of love, for He is speaking to us personally through His Son. God has placed His approval on the message given by Christ, and His divine validation is upon Jesus Himself.

Application

The authors' proposition and proof in Hebrews 1 form an argument that is meant to be persuasive in its entirety, not in any single element. It is a recitation of Christological themes born of pastoral concern. It reiterates the common faith of the audience, explicating it so that only one conclusion can be drawn. Those who find themselves in a challenging, hostile world are aware that they have an unchanging exalted Lord, and even angels are their servants. The author invites his audience to join him in the only fitting response to the Son's enthronement: worship!

HEBREWS 1 I

DO NOT IGNORE THE SON'S MESSAGE

A Warning to Pay Attention

> Therefore we ought to give the more earnest heed to the things which we have heard, lest at any time we should let them slip. For if the word spoken by angels was stedfast, and every transgression and disobedience received a just recompence of reward; How shall we escape, if we neglect so great salvation; which at the first began to be spoken by the Lord, and was confirmed unto us by them that heard him; God also bearing them witness, both with signs and wonders, and with divers miracles, and gifts of the Holy Ghost, according to his own will?
> —Hebrews 2:1-4

THE AUTHOR'S SHORT opening assertion in verse 1 is expanded in one long sentence in verses 2-4. This opening conditional statement, in the form of an *a fortiori* argument, climaxes in a rhetorical question followed by dependent clauses that elaborate on the "great salvation" that the author's audience has received.

The reference to the serving role of angels (see 1:14) echoes the theme of their subservience and the key word "salvation" (see 2:3). The author's brief exhortation draws a conclusion from the argument of chapter 1, but he also connects the transcendent dignity of the Son over the angels, and His subjection of them. The community has to draw the conclusion from its own profession of faith.

The writer shows the appeal to heed what the Son reveals with the help of two images: one nautical, the other legal. The verb "pay attention" ("earnest heed" in the KJV) is an idiomatic expression for listening carefully, but it can also mean to bring a ship to port. More explicit is the verb "to drift away" ("let slip" in the KJV); it suggests the image of a ship without moorings. Salvation has come to the readers as a message for people to "hear." Failure to listen will result in the loss of a secure anchorage.

Promulgation of a law makes it legally valid or binding, and any transgression is an offence requiring a just penalty. That was the case with the giving of the Law at Mount Sinai, and the word spoken by the Son is no less binding. Neglect of His message by deliberate transgression or through disobedience places one under the living God who sees all and judges justly. Greater revelation requires keener hearing and sterner punishment where there is disobedience. The author points out the validity of the message of salvation in three words, "bearing them witness" (2:4), outlining the way in which the sacred tradition has reached the audience. The Proclaimer then became the Proclaimed in the preaching of those who heard Him.

God's tangible witness to the gospel's truth and power are shown in the phrase "according to his own will" (2:5). This qualifies the three ways in which God has provided corroborating evidence:

DO NOT IGNORE THE SON'S MESSAGE

1. "Signs and wonders" is a fixed phrase for God's mighty acts of deliverance. Miracles accompanied the preaching of the gospel in the early church.
2. "Divers miracles" are evidence of God's power at work, as in Jesus' ministry.
3. "Gifts of the Holy Ghost" are the gifts God has provided to His people. The author of Hebrews will not mention gifts of the Spirit again—his concern is the certainty of the message of salvation.

The message of salvation is *the* word from God, the proclamation of Christ, the continuation of primal testimony, and is accompanied by the Spirit's powerful working.

Throughout his letter, the author of Hebrews will call on his audience not to neglect the Word. To do so would be to deny the speaking and acting of God the Father, God the Son, and God the Holy Spirit. It would also deny the development of a Trinitarian theology. The concern of the author is to proclaim Christ, and his repeated appeals to listen and cling to the word shows his concern about a real threat to the lives of his readers and their spiritual indifference. Their hold on the word is not firm, according to what they received.

The Temporary Abasement of the Son

In Hebrews 2:6-8, the author again uses a quotation to describe the nature of Jesus' abasement, citing other texts to amplify the salvific purpose of the Son's identification with humanity. Christological exposition brings the author back to scriptural argument. The superiority of the Son over the angels backed the first set of quotations the author used in Hebrews 1:5-13. In parallel fashion, references to angels bracket the next text cited to show the nature and necessity of the Son's temporary lowliness:

> For unto the angels hath he not put in subjection the world to come, whereof we speak. But one in a certain place testified, saying, What is man, that thou art mindful of him? Or the son of man, that thou visitest him? Thou madest him a little lower than the angels; thou crownedst him with glory and honour, and didst set him over the works of thy hands: Thou hast put all things in subjection under his feet. For in that he put all in subjection under him, he left nothing that is not put under him. But now we see not yet all things put under him. But we see Jesus, who was made a little lower than the angels for the suffering of death, crowned with glory and honour; that he by the grace of God should taste death for every man.
> —Hebrews 2:5-9

Links between Hebrews 2:5-9 and the preceding sections provide reference to the angels, the subjection of everything under the Son's "feet," and the "coming" world that is the focus of future salvation (which repeats a verb expressing futurity). The assertion that God did not subject the coming world to angels (see 2:5) assumes that they have some dominion. God gave the angels oversight of the world's nations, reserving for Himself the care of ministry directed to the future, but only the Son is regent over the "world to come."

The final assertion of the Son's superiority over angels introduces the great paradox: the glorified King was once a lowly human being. The text the author uses here is from Psalm 8:4-6:

> What is man, that thou art mindful of him? And the son of man, that thou visitest him? For thou hast made him

DO NOT IGNORE THE SON'S MESSAGE

a little lower than the angels, and hast crowned him with glory and honour. Thou madest him to have dominion over the works of thy hands: thou hast put all things under his feet.

This psalm speaks of God's act of "subjecting" all things under humanity and illustrates a paradox (these texts are linked elsewhere in the New Testament to depict the results of Christ's exaltation). The psalmist praises the majestic name of God by recalling the exalted status of human beings as creatures who are little less than angels when it comes to having dominion over God's other creatures. The text becomes a prophecy of Christ's temporary humility before His glorification.

For the author of Hebrews, the twin themes of temporary lowliness and final glorification are enough to suggest a Christological application. That God made no exceptions of finiteness—of subjection to death and the fear of death—belies humanity's divine mandate to rule. The fact that humans do "not yet" see humanity's dominion suggests that there will be a time when it will be apparent.

The lack of literal fulfillment suggests to the writer of Hebrews that the true meaning of Psalm 8:4-6 is found elsewhere. Christ is the only one to whom the psalm fully applies, not as the "Son of Man" in terms of a christological title, but as "Representative Human Being." Only this human being was made lower than the angels, though lowliness was not His natural state. By placing the phrase "for a little while" (NASB) before the verb, the author stresses the fact that His humiliation was only for a moment.

We can only say of Jesus that He is now "crowned . . . with glory and honor." His coronation is the fitting reward for His perfect obedience in suffering: He was uniquely representative. His humility, suffering and death were part of a divine plan grounded in the "grace of God." Jesus Christ tasted death for everyone in a vicarious sense. His enthronement as universal ruler corresponds to the universal significance of His suffering. Hebrew's picture of Christ as the representative of humanity brings us close to the Pauline concept of Christ as the last Adam. This second representative, Christ, has everything subjected under Him, including death. For Paul, Christ's resurrection is the key to understanding His present lordship.

The Son's Solidarity with Humanity

> For it became him, for whom are all things, and by whom are all things, in bringing many sons unto glory, to make the captain of their salvation perfect through sufferings. For both he that sanctifieth and they who are sanctified are all of one: for which cause he is not ashamed to call them brethren, saying, I will declare thy name unto my brethren, in the midst of the church will I sing praise unto thee. And again, I will put my trust in him. And again, Behold I and the children which God hath given me. Forasmuch then as the children are partakers of flesh and blood, he also himself likewise took part of the same; that through death he might destroy him that had the power of death, that is, the devil; and deliver them who through fear of death were all their lifetime subject to bondage. For verily he took not on him the nature of angels; but he took on him the seed of Abraham. Wherefore in all things it behoved him to be made like unto his brethren, that he might be a merciful and faithful high priest in things pertaining to God, to make reconciliation for the sins of the people. For in that he himself hath suffered being tempted, he is able to succour them that are tempted.
> —Hebrews 2:10-18

DO NOT IGNORE THE SON'S MESSAGE

Hebrews 2:5-9 depicts the Son as representing humanity in His temporary abasement and present glory. Links between verses 9-10 indicate that a prior argument is being continued: God is the subject in verse 10, though He is identified with a circumlocution; "everyone" in verse 9 is restated with "many sons" in verse 10; the key words "glory" and suffering" are repeated in each verse. To the author, the Son's identification with humanity is fitting and appropriate; His incarnation is in light of what finally happened to Him; those with whom He identifies are children, brothers and sisters; and His sufferings find their counterpart in the sufferings of the readers.

The writer draws a theological conclusion about the appropriateness of God's action in light of verse 9 by saying that it was "fitting" for God to bring the Son to glory through suffering. The author does not recall Paul's doctrine of adoption through the indwelling of the Spirit; rather, he states that human beings are God's children because the Son identifies with them. To lead His children to glory, God brought the first leader to His end (or goal) through suffering. He who was perfect brought others to the goal of their faith. Christ reached the goal that God had set for Him by being installed as heavenly High Priest, but this occurred only after He had been equipped for this role in the school of suffering. Because the Son's "perfection" has cultic connotations, it is natural that His solidarity with God's children should also be expressed in cultic terms. The Son sanctifies people through His self-sacrifice, so that they are consecrated and "perfected" for priestly access to God and sacrifice of praise.

In verse 11, we find the Son's confession to His human siblings; He is "not ashamed to call them brethren." The fact that Jesus was "not ashamed" suggests an eagerness to acknowledge or accept; God was not ashamed to be the God of the patriarchs, while Moses was ashamed to be identified as the son of Pharaoh's daughter.

The Son's first confession in verse 12 is part of the suffering saint's cry for help. He recalls occasions when God comes to his rescue and changes his song of woe to one of praise. Two factors most likely prompted the writer of Hebrews to place these words into the Son's mouth. First, in the passion tradition, Jesus identified Himself with the psalmist by taking on His own lips the opening words of this psalm: "My God, my God why have you forsaken me?" (Psalm 22:1). Second, the Greek word for "assembly" (*ekklesia*) is the normal word translated as "church."

In verses 13-14, the author quotes from Isaiah 8:17 and 18. Like the psalmist, Isaiah speaks as one who has endured suffering; in his case, his suffering came through the people's rejection of his message. He sees himself and his children (including his disciples) as a sign of hope at a time when foreign invasion looms on the horizon. Isaiah's description of the children as God's gift suggests the final purpose of His solidarity with them: to lead them from suffering and death to glory. They are not merely his children by virtue of belonging to the human family, but because they belong to the family of faith.

The author of Hebrews places the goal of this identification in a chiastic formulation: through His death, Christ disempowered the one who has the power of death (the parenthetical naming of the devil falls outside the neat structure). The writer presupposes that Jesus Christ, the perfect sacrifice, has effectively removed sin as the root cause of human mortality. He also presupposes that the power of death is overcome by the power of an indestructible life. In Greek literature, the experience of mortality meant being subjected to a lifelong slavery to fear. By remaining the trusting and obedient Son, Jesus delivered His siblings

DO NOT IGNORE THE SON'S MESSAGE

from the fear of death, and He remains their champion when life-threatening situations tempt them to surrender their trust.

Verse 16 marks the end of the author's scriptural argument. He also identifies the beneficiaries of the Son's work of deliverance through a final comparison involving the angels who are not "flesh and blood." The "fear not" summons and the reminders that help come from God are echoes in the portrayal of Christ. All who inherit the promise of God and trustingly cling to them are descendants of Abraham.

Application

The author of Hebrews intends every reference to Christ's once-for-all sacrifice and entry into the heavenly sanctuary to be part of a statement about His ongoing work as exalted High Priest. Christ, as the exalted High Priest, provides continual cleansing from sin through the application of His blood, and He can do so because He lives forever. Thus, the high-priestly title found in Hebrews 2:17 introduces two features of His present work: cleansing people from sin and interceding for sinners.

HEBREWS III

THE SUPERIOR FAITHFULNESS OF THE SON

The Son, as Faithful High Priest, Calls to Faith

> Wherefore, holy brethren, partakers of the heavenly calling, consider the Apostle and High Priest of our profession, Christ Jesus; who was faithful to him that appointed him, as also Moses was faithful in all his house. For this man was counted worthy of more glory than Moses, inasmuch as he who hath builded the house hath more honour than the house. For every house is builded by some man; but he that built all things is God.
>
> —Hebrews 3:1-4

THE THEMATIC UNITY of Hebrews 3:1-4 and 13 centers on the concepts of faithfulness and obedience. In this passage, the author makes a new comparison between the Son and Moses to demonstrate the superior faithfulness of the Son. His call for the hearers to remain faithful leads to the portrayal of Israel's disobedience.

These verses are expository. The writer makes his argument on scriptural allusions rather than direct quotations;

the key words being "faithful," "priest" and "house." He structures his argument as follows:

1. An opening appeal establishes the terms of reference for him to make a comparison between Jesus Christ and Moses (3:1-2).
2. He uses an analogy of the relationship of the builder to what he builds to demonstrate the superiority of Jesus Christ (3:3-4).
3. He shows how Jesus is faithful as a Son over God's house (3:5-6).
4. He forms a conclusion with parenetic implications (3:6).

It is natural that an argument demonstrating the Son's superiority to Moses should follow the argument for the Son's ranking above angels. For the author, Moses was the true representative of the prophets through whom God spoke in the past through angels. He recognizes the unique mediatory role of Moses in establishing the Sinaitic covenant. Although Moses was called a priest in Psalms and was the son of a Levite couple, he interceded in priestly fashion for Israel and altered his function.

Faith focuses on Jesus, who completed the course. His earthly name recalls that He became human to be like His siblings. His name remains Jesus in His exaltation, no matter what other titles He receives.

The precise content and original setting of the "confession" in verse 1 are not stated. It may have included a reference to Christ as High Priest but had its focus on the Son. The title "apostle" and "high priest" belong together, as both suggest divine authorization and appointment. The Son is the authoritative emissary who reveals God's will in the last times. "Apostle" is placed first probably because it

THE SUPERIOR FAITHFULNESS OF THE SON

describes the movement from God to humanity, whereas "high priest" embraces the movement from earthly suffering to heavenly installation.

The Analogy of the Builder

> And Moses verily was faithful in all his house, as a servant, for a testimony of those things which were to be spoken after; but Christ as a son over his own house; whose house are we, if we hold fast the confidence and the rejoicing of the hope firm unto the end.
> —Hebrews 3:5-6

As great as Moses was, an even greater One with a greater mission appears. Consequently, God ascribes more glory to Him than to Moses. The author's analogy suggested by the word "house" shows this to be entirely fitting. This is a truism: a builder who designs and erects a house deserves greater honor than the construction itself. God, as Creator, is the builder of all things, including the house of Israel.

The Argument Concerning Status: Moses was faithful in God's house as a servant. He was a trusted and faithful intimate of God, yet he remained only a servant of the household. By contrast, the faithfulness of Christ (the title appears here for the first time in Hebrews) was over God's house as a Son. The author does not place this in the past tense but present tense, indicating that Christ continues to fulfill this role.

The Conclusion: The picture of Christ as royal priest determines the sense in which the audience is God's house. The texts speak of the establishment of a new priestly house and a new royal house, both of which will last forever. Christ fulfils both hopes in that He is now a High Priest and a Son. Confidence and hope are essential marks of God's purified and consecrated people.

In Hebrews 3:6, the author states, "we hold fast the confidence and the rejoicing of the hope firm unto the end." The term in the Greek for "confidence" (*parresia*) originally suggested the freedom of citizens to speak their mind; it is associated in Hebrews with confession to Christ, who opens access to the heavenly sanctuary and allows us to address God freely and confidently. "Pride that belong[s] to hope" (NRSV) means the content of boasting that gives hope. The inference is clear: we need to cling to the confession of Christ as faithful Son and High Priest.

Whatever the connotations behind the phrase "God's house," the audience saw in it as an apt description of their own situation as members of a house church. "House" describes a concrete reality as well as an image. It suggests intimacy, protection, solidarity and unity. Loss of confidence and hope means losing that which binds the family of God together.

The Faithlessness of Israel in the Wilderness

In the next passage, the author uses a homiletic midrash on Psalm 95, which itself interprets the exodus story in light of Numbers 14, to provide a negative example of Israel's faithlessness in the wilderness. He does this to show that what was once true for the desert generation now applies to the present readers.

> Wherefore (as the Holy Ghost saith, today if ye will hear his voice, harden not your hearts, as in the provocation, in the day of temptation in the wilderness: when your fathers tempted me, proved me, and saw my works forty years. Wherefore I was grieved with that generation, and said, They do always err in their heart; and they have not known my ways. So I sware in my wrath, They shall not enter into my rest.) Take heed, brethren, lest there

THE SUPERIOR FAITHFULNESS OF THE SON

be in any of you an evil heart of unbelief, in departing from the living God. But exhort one another daily, while it is called today; lest any of you be hardened through the deceitfulness of sin. For we are made partakers of Christ, if we hold the beginning of our confidence stedfast unto the end; while it is said, Today if ye will hear His voice, harden not your hearts, as in the provocation. For some when they had heard, did provoke: howbeit not all that came out of Egypt by Moses. But with whom was he grieved forty years? Was it not with them that had sinned, whose carcasses fell in the wilderness? And to whom sware he that they should not enter into his rest, but to them that believed not? So we see that they could not enter in because of unbelief.
—Hebrews 3:7-19

Psalm 95 contains an invitation to worship God, followed by a call to hear His voice and obey. At Rephidim, the people provoked God to anger by complaining about the shortage of water. Moses named the place Massah (meaning "trial") and Meribah (meaning "quarrel" or "strife").

The focus of the psalmist (and our writer), however, is on the rebellion at Kedesh, when the Israelites, despite seeing God's glory and signs of deliverance in the exodus, refused to enter the land that God had promised to them. God's answer to the rebellion was to prohibit those who tested His patience by not listening to His voice from entering into the land that He had swore to them. Of the host of people who left Egypt, only Caleb and Joshua survived to enter the land. In formulating God's complaint—they always go astray in their hearts—the psalmist is thinking of Israel's persistent refusal to accept God's directions and promises.

Disregarding minor changes, Hebrews alters "this" to "that generation" in verse 10, thereby making it clear that the Spirit is talking about God's anger against Israel in the past. The writer also links the "forty years" with Israel seeing God's work in the desert, though he later returns to the original connection in verse 17. By linking the forty years with God's signs, the author wants to highlight "divine grace," which leaves the promise in verse 11 open.

Application

Heeding the Spirit's warnings is a matter of familial responsibility, so we need continuous and mutual encouragement. The concept of unbelief reflects Israel's refusal to believe, while the heart as "evil" recalls the description of Israel itself as wicked. By repeating the opening word "today," the writer stresses that the word of warning and promise still applies in the present day of salvation. Partnership with Christ exists only where there is certainty of faith. The text speaks, literally, of the need to cling to the "beginning" of confidence until the "end," thus suggesting the path that Christ follows as the pioneer perfecta of faith. Perseverance and patient endurance are required to reach the promised rest.

Hebrews IV

THE PROMISE OF FINAL REST

O come, let us sing unto the Lord: let us make a joyful noise to the rock of our salvation. Let us come before his presence with thanksgiving, and make a joyful noise unto him with psalms. For the Lord is a great God, and a great King above all gods. In his hand are the deep places of the earth: the strength of the hills is his also. The sea is his, and he made it: and his hands formed the dry land. O come, let us worship and bow down: let us kneel before the Lord our maker. For he is our God; and we are the people of his pasture, and the sheep of his hand. Today if ye will hear his voice, harden not your heart, as in the provocation, and as in the day of temptation in the wilderness: when your fathers tempted me, proved me, and saw my work. Forty years long was I grieved with this generation, and said, It is a people that do err in their heart, and they have not known my ways: Unto whom I sware in my wrath that they should not enter into my rest.

—Psalm 95:1-11

THE COMPASSIONATE GOD

BEHIND THE AUTHOR'S positive application of Psalm 95 lie two basic assumptions: (1) God's promises remain valid despite human faithlessness, and (2) God's word can never remain unfulfilled. Israel's disobedience and unbelief did not invalidate the promise of rest; they just refused to claim it. Canaan was extended to the children of the wilderness generation.

Special Diligence Is Needed to Enter God's Rest

> Let us therefore fear, lest, a promise being left us of entering into his rest, any of you should seem to come short of it. For unto us was the gospel preached, as well as unto them: but the word preached did not profit them, not being mixed with faith in them that heard it. For we which have believed do enter into rest, as he said, As I have sworn in my wrath, if they shall enter into my rest: although the works were finished from the foundation of the world. For he spake in a certain place of the seventh day on this wise, and God did rest the seventh day from all his works. And in this place again, if they shall enter into my rest.
> —Hebrews 4:1-5

Special diligence is now needed so that no one loses out on the full effects of the promise given as a creative word. Note that though the verb "to announce good news" occurs twice in verses 2 and 6, the noun "gospel" did not actually appear in Hebrews. The related etymological word that replaced it is "promise" in 4:1. The good news is a promissory that holds out the prospect of a future inheritance that believers can claim by faith. Faith was the condition for appropriating the promise in the past, and it is the condition for appropriating it now. Israel received the good news of a promised rest but forfeited the land through disobedience, which is a lack of faith. Verse 3 develops the contrast between "we who have believed" and the unbelieving generation whom God debarred from entering the Promised Land.

The author's second purpose for repeating Psalm 95:11 in verse 3 is to define the word "rest": it is God's own rest that He has enjoyed since "the foundation of the world." The objection that "rest" refers to that which God entered and not the land of Canaan is countered in verses 3-5 by linking Psalm 95:11, "Unto whom I sware in my wrath that they should not enter into my rest," with Genesis 2:2, "And on the seventh day God ended his work which he had made: and he rested on the seventh day from all his work which he had made." The latter verse speaks of God resting from His work of creation on the seventh day. The point is that God's own resting from the work of creation is an archetype for the final rest promised to Christians. It is a common early Jewish and Christian argument that an original state of affairs retains validity over that which comes later. For instance, the priesthood of Melchizadek is above that of Levi, since it precedes it.

The argument used in Hebrews 4:3-5 is similar to the previous one; God's own original, archetypal rest determines how the promise of eschatological rest for His creatures is to be understood. Because God's rest precedes human history, the final rest cannot be on the plane of normal human history as a restored home in earthly land.

A Call to Labor to Enter into Final Rest

> Seeing therefore it remaineth that some must enter therein, and they to whom it was first preached entered not in because of unbelief: Again, he limiteth a certain day, saying in David, Today, after so long a time; as it is said, Today if ye will hear his voice, harden not your

hearts. For if Jesus had given them rest, then would he not afterward have spoken of another day. There remaineth therefore a rest to the people of God. For he that is entered into his rest, he also hath ceased from his own works, as God did from his. Let us labour therefore to enter into that rest, lest any man fall after the same example of unbelief.

—Hebrews 4:6-11

In verses 6-11, we see that the author's sweeping condemnation of a past generation's disobedience is to show the availability of the promise to another generation. Heavenly rest is not a gift for a selected few but for the whole people of God. David is specifically stated to be the agent of the prophetic word in order to stress the great time gap between the Exodus and the "today" that falls much later. There is a distinction between the "days of resting" found in Psalm 95:8—"Harden not your heart, as in the provocation, and as in the day of temptation in the wilderness"—and the "today" of Psalm 95:7—"For he is our God; and we are the people of his pasture, and the sheep of his hand. Today if ye will hear his voice." David, a person of faith, is speaking about a day in the future, one that arrived in the salvation offered in Jesus Christ. Although the name "Joshua" in Greek is "Jesus," the author does not offer a comparison between Joshua, who did not lead the people to their final rest, and Jesus, who now leads the people to their final rest.

So far, the writer has used a word for "rest" (*katapausis*) that has land associations. In verse 9, he now uses a new word (*sabbatismos*) to imply the observation of Sabbath as an act of worship in praise of God. Those who enjoy this rest have a Sabbath celebration that conforms to God's own resting. The analogy with God's own rest is complete in itself; it does not require us to identify the "labors" from

THE PROMISE OF FINAL REST

which believers rest, whether the trials and temptations of life generally or specific persecutions. The writer is working a concept that acquires varying associations within a long tradition of Old Testament and Jewish thought. Rest is synonymous with the eternal inheritance of salvation to which believers look in hope. As the consummation of Christian hope, the final rest is the believer's glorification with Christ—their perfection and their citizenship in an abiding city, in a heavenly country, and an unshakeable kingdom. The author's stress on rest as promised and his appeal for believers to strive to enter it suggests that rest is a future reality. This tension between present fulfillment and future realization is not resolved, but it can be understood by noting the worship themes that underlie the author's thinking. Hebrews 4:9-10 anticipates the festival of the priestly people of God in the heavenly sanctuary, celebrating the eternal Sabbath in the presence of God with unceasing praise and adoration.

Do Not Reject The Word of God

> For the word of God is quick, and powerful, and sharper than any twoedged sword, piercing even to the dividing asunder of soul and spirit, and of the joints and marrow, and is a discerner of the thoughts and intents of the heart. Neither is there any creature that is not manifest in his sight: but all things are naked and opened unto the eyes of him with whom we have to do.
> —Hebrews 4:12-13

God's Word is powerful in effecting what it promises and judging disobedience. The author makes this point by using descriptions of the word derived from the Old Testament and from other Wisdom traditions:

1. God's Word is living because it comes from the living God. Because the Hebrew speaks of the living God as judge, the point here is not the life-giving power of the word but its ability to expose and judge sin.
2. The depiction of the Word as a sharp sword is a traditional image. In Isaiah 49:2, the prophet states, "And he hath made my mouth like a sharp sword; in the shadow of his hand hath he hid me, and made me a polished shaft; in his quiver hath he hid me." Paul depicts the word as the sword of the Spirit, the two-edged sword.
3. The Word penetrates into a person's innermost being in a way that no knife or sword can do. The division of the soul from the spirit and the joints from the marrow is not made to define the psychological and physiological composition of humanity but to picture the deep recesses of people's spiritual and physical being into which the word can penetrate.
4. God's Word judges in the sense that it critically discerns secret thoughts and intentions. God alone knows human hearts and can separate genuine from false.

The author can easily move from the Word of God to God in verse 13 because the word bears God's own attributes. God's all-seeing eye renders all creatures exposed and defenseless. People must give account to God, who speaks the word to them.

According to the writer, all theology that speaks about God and speaks to God begins with the Word. By including himself in the warning, he shows his awareness of his own accountability. Therefore, any unfaithfulness on his part will incur the judgment of the Word. His main focus is on those who are the object of this pastoral concern. The Word of promise can become the Word of judgment.

THE PROMISE OF FINAL REST

Major Appeal: Hold Your Confession and Draw Near to God

The author's plea for immovable firmness in confessing Christ is complemented by another plea that suggests movement to God's throne:

> Seeing then that we have a great high priest, that is passed into the heavens, Jesus the Son of God, let us hold fast our profession. For we have not an high priest which cannot be touched with the feeling of our infirmities; but was in all points tempted like as we are, yet without sin. Let us therefore come boldly unto the throne of grace, that we may obtain mercy, and find grace to help in time of need.
> —Hebrews 4:14-16

The basis for each plea is in verses 14 and 15. The second appeal concludes by stating the reason why believers can have bold access into God's presence: the offices of the merciful High Priest ensured the reception of mercy. Hebrews 4:14-16 represents a first appeal for believers to draw near to God that will be repeated later in Hebrews 10:19-23:

Hebrews 4:14-16	Hebrews 10:19-23
Since we have	Since we have
a great high priest	a great priest
through the heavens	through the curtain
Jesus	Jesus
(the Son) of God	(the house) of God
let us hold fast to our confession	let us hold fast to our confession
let us approach with boldness	let us approach with boldness

First Proposition: The author can closely associate the titles "Son" and "High Priest" because he sees both as designating the status of Jesus in His exaltation, a truth that is stated in Scripture. The writer focuses on Jesus' role as High Priest because it is open to treatment in terms of both His past and present saving activity. Christ is *the* great high priest in an absolute sense, since He is above Aaron and his heirs in the old covenant. He is the ultimate Great Priest. The traditional, cosmic spatial description of Christ's glorification in terms of an ascent equates with what Hebrews elsewhere expresses in cultic imagery as entry into the heavenly sanctuary.

First Appeal: The phrase "since we have" denotes an apprehension of a faith reality that is formally confessed in a creedal statement. The meaning of to "hold fast" to the confession is to cling to Him who is its content.

Second Proposition: The exaltation of Jesus Christ as a Son and High Priest does not mean His removal from the human nature He shares. Like any other human being, Jesus Christ is subject to human weakness. He experienced the agony of suffering and fear of death. He was susceptible to temptation. As one who still shares humanity, Jesus suffers with those who are weak and open to temptation, which is why He can help all of humanity. The great difference between Him and His siblings is that He was and remains without sin. The author is asserting that Jesus Christ never broke faith with God, even in the face of suffering and death.

Second Appeal: Believers can approach God with confidence because they have a compassionate High Priest in God's presence who fully identifies with them in their weakness. Through Jesus Christ's high-priestly work, the throne of God symbolizes the divine majesty and power found in throne of grace. On the Day of Atonement, only the high priest could approach the throne of God's mercy seat in the Holy of Holies. Jesus Christ's finished work of purifying sinners and His ongoing intercession ensure that those who are in need will receive mercy and find grace at the right time.

HEBREWS V

CHRIST QUALIFIED TO BE COMPASSIONATE HIGH PRIEST

Requirements for Office

THE LETTER OF Hebrews establishes Jesus Christ's priesthood on the background of the Old Testament priesthood. Divine appointment and solidarity with those He serves are the two prime qualifications for His office.

> For every high priest taken from among men is ordained for men in things pertaining to God, that he may offer both gifts and sacrifices for sins: Who can have compassion on the ignorant, and on them that are out of the way; for that he himself also is compassed with infirmity. And by reason hereof he ought, as for the people, so also for himself, to offer for sins. And no man taketh this honour unto himself, but he that is called of God, as was Aaron.
> —Hebrews 5:1-4

There are significant parallels in the description of priestly functions in 5:1-3 and the function of Jesus Christ in 7:26-28, as follows:

Hebrews 5:1-3	Hebrews 7:26-28
every high priest	such an high priest
taken from among men	separate from sinners
ordained for men	the word of the oath
offer [self] . . . for sins	this he did once
he himself	for his own sins
as for the people	then for the people's

Note that in both texts, the priests in the old order are subject to weakness. Christ has the ability to suffer with those who are beset by weakness. The Son became like His siblings to endure testing and to suffer with them in their weakness.

Under the old order, the high priest functioned as an intermediary, representing God to humanity and humanity to God. He was chosen from among mortals to act on their behalf, and God put him in charge of his office to act on His behalf. In this capacity, the priest would offer gifts and sacrifice, a parallel to the sacrifices of Yom Kippur, which the author is primarily concerned with here. Divine appointment did not remove the high priest from the common lot.

This was the first requirement for the priest's office. The second requirement was that the priest had to identify with those whom he served. In Leviticus, the high priest is pictured on the Day of Atonement first making sacrifice for himself and his household, and then for the people. Reverting to the theme of divine appointment in verse 4, the author indicates his chief concern: the question of legitimacy.

CHRIST QUALIFIED TO BE COMPASSIONATE HIGH PRIEST

The New High Priest

Continuity between the old and the new order demands that God appoint a new high priest, who will carry out his office in solidarity with humanity. The key christological texts the author uses in verses 5-6 assert this divine appointment:

> I will declare the decree: the LORD hath said unto me, Thou art my Son; this day have I begotten thee.
> —Psalm 2:7

> The LORD hath sworn, and will not repent, Thou art a priest for ever after the order of Melchizedek."
> —Psalm 110:4

Together, these verses are quoted in Hebrew 5:5-6:

> So also Christ glorified not himself to be made an high priest; but he that said unto him, Thou art my Son, today have I begotten thee. As he saith also in another place, Thou art a priest for ever after the order of Melchisedec.

The "today" of Psalm 2:7 is fulfilled in the moment of Jesus' accession in glory. The royal title of Jesus Christ, the "anointed one," suggests that His divine appointment already existed. Verses 5, 6 and 10 complement each other in the same way as verses 1 and 4.

Jesus' Authority to Function as Royal Son

> Who in the days of his flesh, when he had offered up prayers and supplications with strong crying and tears unto him that was able to save him from death, and was heard in that he feared; though he were a Son, yet learned

he obedience by the things which he suffered; and being made perfect, he became the author of eternal salvation unto all them that obey him; called of God an high priest after the order of Melchisedec.

—Hebrews 5:7-10

The issue in these verses is Jesus Christ's installation into an office and His authority to function as the royal Son. His acclamation as Son also means His installation as the heavenly High Priest. The author quotes Psalm 110:4 in verse 6 to form the basis for understanding the uniqueness of the Son's high-priestly office.

In Hebrews 5:7-8, the author returns to his theme in verses 2-3. Christ's identification with mortals in their weakness includes suffering and death. His references to fervent pleas, suffering, death and obedient submission seem to recall the passion story. In Gethsemane, Jesus Christ pleaded to have His suffering removed, yet He submitted to the will of His Father.

The fact that God heard Christ because of His submission is shown by God's sending of an angel to comfort and strengthen Him (see Luke 22:43), as well as the divine voice from heaven that Jesus heard when He was troubled by the prospect of death. Obedient submission in suffering is a necessary prelude to the High Priest's enthronement. He was tested to equip Him for His office as merciful High Priest. The active obedience of the Son produces an eternal salvation, a phrase the author most likely borrowed from Isaiah 45:17: "But Israel shall be saved in the LORD with an everlasting salvation: ye shall not be ashamed nor confounded world without end."

The author then pastorally reminds his readers that the pioneer and perfecter of their faith know their weaknesses,

CHRIST QUALIFIED TO BE COMPASSIONATE HIGH PRIEST

temptations and trials. Because He was once with them in suffering, He can now be for them in their suffering.

A Call to Spiritual Maturity

> Of whom we have many things to say, and hard to be uttered, seeing ye are dull of hearing. For when for the time ye ought to be teachers, ye have need that one teach you again which be the first principles of the oracles of God; and are become such as have need of milk, and not of strong meat. For every one that useth milk is unskillful in the word of righteousness: for he is a babe. But strong meat belongeth to them that are of full age, even those who by reason of use have their senses exercised to discern both good and evil.
> —Hebrews 5:11-14

The author's centerpiece—the exposition of Christ's high priesthood—finds its counterpart in this concluding exhortation. The writer adopts the stance of a teacher who expresses strong regret over his students' lack of progress beyond the basic elements and basic teachings that have provided the foundation for their faith. (The phrase "by this time" in verse 12 shows that his readers are not recent converts.) He states that his theme is difficult to explain not because of his inability as teacher or the difficulty of subject matter, but because his audience has "become dull in understanding" and cannot move on to deeper perceptions.

The use of metaphors such as milk and solid food are common in Hellenistic moral philosophy, especially when describing stages of instruction. In this case, they denote more than the natural diet of the infant and adult; they stand for the difference in the power of discernment between the infant and the mature adult. The phrase "in the word of righteousness" found in verse 13 is a Semitism for "right speech." The writer is using a parallelism of verse 13a and verse 14, stating that the "word of righteousness" equals "strong food" in the sense of instruction, whether doctrinal or ethical, that can be put to the test by experience.

HEBREWS VI

A STRONG WARNING

Progressing to Perfection

DESPITE THE AUTHOR'S frustration that his readers are slow to learn, he assumes that they can progress to perfection and make the distinctions that mature adults can make.

> Therefore leaving the principles of the doctrine of Christ, let us go on unto perfection; not laying again the foundation of repentance from dead works, and of faith toward God, of the doctrine of baptisms, and of laying on of hands, and of resurrection of the dead, and of eternal judgment. And this will we do, if God permit.
> —Hebrews 6:1-3

The elementary teaching about (not of) Christ the author mentions in verse 1 must refer to the first instruction the readers received that brought them to their conversion. This teaching remains foundational for deeper insights into the faith and its practical consequences. This primary instruction in the Christian faith was developed on the basis of the Old Testament—repentance and faith are fundamental elements in conversion. Specifically, the writer calls for the believers to repent from "dead works," by which he means turning away from the old life that led to death—one that the old cultic regulations were powerless to deal with. Faith in God represents the new confidence the believer enjoys in worshiping the living God.

Instruction about "the doctrine of baptisms" refers to the old purification rites that could effect only an external cleansing; the perfect washing is found in the blood of Jesus Christ and the water of baptism. Instruction concerning the "laying on of hands" refers to confirming the gifts of the Spirit. Christian instruction in eschatology—the "resurrection of the dead" and "eternal judgment"—concentrates on Jesus Christ. Finally, the author's phrase "if God permits" acknowledges that the attainment of such maturity depends on God's blessing.

A Warning Against Rejecting the Son

> For it is impossible for those who were once enlightened, and have tasted of the heavenly gift, and were made partakers of the Holy Ghost, and have tasted the good word of God, and the powers of the world to come, if they shall fall away, to renew them again unto repentance; seeing they crucify to themselves the Son of God afresh, and put him to an open shame. For the earth which drinketh in the rain that cometh oft upon it, and bringeth forth herbs meet for them by whom it is dressed, receiveth blessing from God: but that which beareth thorns and briers is rejected, and is nigh unto cursing; whose end is to be burned.
> —Hebrews 6:4-8

A STRONG WARNING

The "enlightenment" the author mentions in verse 4 describes the first experience of the gospel that sets the convert's life in a new direction. The image of light suggests both new knowledge and a new way of life, and there are allusions to baptism in verses 4-5. The author then states that in contrast to the reception of God's good gifts stands the dreadful possibility of absolute and final rejection. Those who reject the Son, the writer says, cannot be restored to repentance (see v. 6). The logic of this declaration, which has caused problems for both the early church and modern commentators, is found in the total argument of 6:1-6. It is an absolute, unqualified statement, not to be reduced to rhetorical hyperbole in order to rescue God's boundless grace from limitation.

"Apostasy" means self-exclusion from renewal and faith. In verse 7, the writer uses an agricultural image with scriptural overtones to illustrate the difference between faith and apostasy and between divine approval and final judgment. God originally blessed the land so that it would produce crops. After the Fall, however, He placed a curse on the land to bear thorns and thistles. Israel was God's vineyard that He carefully cultivated, but when it failed to produce fruit, God condemned it to growing briars and thorns. A community of faith is like a field that soaks in the rain and produces good crops. It thrives on God's gifts and care and continues to be a blessing. Conversely, a faithless community will produce the noxious growth consigned to the fire (a symbol of eschatological judgment), and the threat of God's curse will hang over the apostate community itself.

A Word of Encouragement

> But beloved, we are persuaded better things of you, and things that accompany salvation, thou we thus speak. For God is not unrighteous to forget your work and labour of love which ye have shown toward his name, in that ye have ministered to the saints, and do minister. And we desire that every one of you do show the same diligence to the full assurance of hope unto the end: That ye be not slothful, but followers of them who through faith and patience inherit the promises.
> —Hebrews 6:9-12

In Hebrews 6:4-6, the author gives a stern warning of the dire consequences of abandoning the only foundation there is for repentance and faith. Yet despite the author's fears for the spiritual welfare of his "beloved," the community's past practice of love is a matter of record, and he has confidence in them. The acts of love they have done for God's sake continue into the present. "Full assurance of hope" is an extension into the future of full assurance of faith. By inviting his readers to be imitators, he adopts the stance of the teacher.

The Certainty of God's Promises

> For when God made promise to Abraham, because he could swear by no greater, he sware by himself, saying, Surely blessing I will bless thee, and multiplying I will multiply thee. And so, after he had patiently endured, he obtained the promise. For men verily swear by the greater: and an oath for confirmation is to them an end of all strife. Wherein God, willing more abundantly to show unto the heirs of promise the immutability of his counsel, confirmed it by an oath: That by two immutable things, in which it was impossible for God to lie, we might

have a strong consolation, who have fled for refuge to lay hold upon the hope set before us: which hope we have as an anchor of the soul, both sure and stedfast, and which entereth into that within the veil; whither the forerunner is for us entered, even Jesus, made an high priest for ever after the order of Melchisedec.

—Hebrews 6:13-20

The author's references to God's promise to Abraham and to Abraham as a paradigm of faith provide linguistic and thematic links with the preceding parenesis. Abraham is an obvious prototype for those who call themselves his descendants, and the prominence that the author of Hebrews gives to the patriarch reflects Abraham's standing in ancient Jewish and Christian thought. After showing unquestionable readiness to obey God's command to sacrifice Isaac, the son of promise, Abraham received a confirmation and extension of earlier promises of blessing.

Regarding the importance of the sacrifice of Isaac in the early synagogue and church, the writer sees the oath as both proving the reliability of a divine promise and as providing encouragement to believers to take hold of the promise of God. The author is aware of the tension between the promise and the fulfillment of that promise in the story of Abraham. Although Isaac was born as promised, and although God promised immense blessing after Isaac's rescue from death, Abraham lived without seeing fulfillment of that promise in the form of many descendants and possession of an earthly land. Abraham "obtained the promise" only after living his whole life as an example of patient endurance.

To take an "oath" meant to call on a higher authority to attest the truth of a statement. Old Testament law required that oaths be sworn only "before the Lord" and "by his name" (see Deuteronomy 6:13) Abraham called on God in this way. Another denotation is that the taking of an oath confirms the truth of a statement in any debate. The author cites God's oath to Abraham in order to point to an imperative oath that is still valid. The heirs of the promise are Abraham's immediate descendants, but believers are the ones who inherit the promises. There is no one greater by whom to swear other than God Himself.

Notice the parallel between 6:13-20 and 7:17-21:

> For he testifieth, Thou art a Priest for ever after the order of Melchisedec. For there is verily a disannulling of the commandment going before for the weakness and unprofitableness thereof. For the law made nothing perfect, but the bringing in of a better hope did; by the which we draw nigh unto God. And inasmuch as not without an oath he was made priest: (For those priests were made without an oath; but this with an oath by him that said unto him, The Lord sware and will not repent, Thou art a priest for ever after the order of Melchisedec.)

This suggests that the author thinks of the declaration of the Son as High Priest. The oath is the guarantee that His will is constant and not fickle.

Application

The two unchangeable things demonstrate the unchangeableness of God's purpose, but the first text is both promise and oath.

Just as the high priest on Yom Kippur passed through the curtain that separated the Holy Place from the Holy of Holies, so Jesus Christ passed through the veil separating us from the innermost sanctuary of God's presence. The phrase "on our behalf" alludes to His perfect sacrifice for all sin as well as to His office of continual intercession. And

A STRONG WARNING

because Jesus enters into the inner shrine behind the curtain and into the heavenly sanctuary on our behalf, we have hope that provides stability and assurance in the storms of life. Our Christian hope is firmly anchored to God's own throne, to which the Son has been exalted as Melchizedek High Priest.

HEBREWS VII

THE SUPERIORITY OF MELCHIZEDEK AS HIGH PRIEST

THE AUTHOR'S EXPOSITION in this chapter takes the form of homiletic midrash. The author works with typology: Melchizedek becomes a type or model of Christ. Note that in verse 1 and 10 the author mentions Melchizedek meeting Abraham; this is actually the king of Sodom who meets the patriarch (see Genesis 14:17: "And they returned, and came to Enmishpat, which is Kadesh, and smote all the country of the Amalekites, and also the Amorites, that dwelt in Hazezontamar)." This forms an inclusion.

The Meeting

The story of the meeting between Melchizedek and Abraham is told in Genesis 14:17-20:

> And the king of Sodom went out to meet him after his return from the slaughter of Chedorlaomer, and of the kings that were with him, at the valley of Shaveh, which is the king's dale. And Melchizedek king of Salem

brought forth bread and wine: and he was the priest of the most high God. And he blessed him, and said, Blessed be Abram of the most high God, possessor of heaven and earth: And blessed be the most high God, which hath delivered thine enemies into thy hand. And he gave him tithes of all.
—Genesis 14:17-20

The writer highlights this meeting between Melchizedek and Abraham by citing key phrases from the story:

For this Melchisedec, king of Salem, priest of the most high God, who met Abraham returning from the slaughter of the kings, and blessed him; to whom also Abraham gave a tenth part of all; first being by interpretation King of righteousness, and after that also King of Salem, which is, King of peace; without father, without mother, without descent, having neither beginning of days, nor end of life; but made like unto the Son of God abideth a priest continually.
—Hebrews 7:1-3

In the story, Abraham, returning home from pursuing and defeating the foreign kings who captured his nephew Lot, received a blessing from the king of Salem, who came out of the city bearing gifts of bread and wine. In return, Abraham gave Melchizedek a tenth of the spoils of war. The author is interested only in the *person* and not the *meaning* of Salem, which is Jerusalem. Only the mysterious Melchizedek and the implications of giving a blessing and receiving a tithe is important.

The name and title of Melchizedek have special significance; "King of righteousness" and "King of peace" have popular etymologies. Righteousness and peace are marks of the age of the Messiah. In Israel and early Judaism, the right

THE SUPERIORITY OF MELCHIZEDEK AS HIGH PRIEST

to exercise priestly functions depended on an unbroken ancestral record. After the exile, the issue of legitimacy for the priesthood on the basis of Levitical lineage became a key issue. That Melchizedek is "without descent" means there is no record of his priestly lineage. In what sense is he "without father, without mother"? Because his birth and death are not recorded, he has neither beginning of days nor end of days.

A reading of Hebrews 7:3, which turns Melchizedek into a superhuman figure, seems to run counter to the author's stress on the uniqueness of Jesus Christ. However, Melchizedek's lack of lineage simply marks him as belonging to a different order of priesthood. He remains a priest forever only as an antitype that foreshadows an eternal priesthood. Melchizedek is a typological model, deliberately brought into the biblical narrative to point to the only one who truly remains a priest forever.

The Meaning of the Two Actions

The author draws certain conclusions from the actions of Abraham and Melchizedek in the Genesis narrative. His aim here is to prove how great Melchizedek is in terms of his absolute superiority over a later order of priests that descended from Abraham.

> Now consider how great this man was, unto whom even the patriarch Abraham gave the tenth of the spoils. And verily they that are of the sons of Levi, who receive the office of the priesthood, have a commandment to take tithes of the people according to the law, that is, of their brethren, though they come out of the loins of Abraham: but he whose descent is not counted from them received tithes of Abraham, and blessed him that had the promises. And without all contraction the less is blessed of the

better. And here men that die receive tithes; but there he receiveth them, of whom it is witnessed that he liveth. And as I may so say, Levi also, who receiveth tithes, paid tithes in Abraham. For he was yet in the loins of his father, when Melchisedec met him.
—Hebrews 7:4-10

For the author of Hebrews, Abraham's payment to Melchizedek of a tenth of his war booty has a connotation beyond the surface meaning of the text. He does not receive the tithe from Abraham as a representative of the Levitical priesthood; in fact, he does not even belong to the descendants of the patriarch. He is without their genealogy. The argument, therefore, is that Melchizedek's priesthood is superior because of the blessing he gave to Abraham. According to this principle, that which is older or original is more authoritative and enduring. The author's conclusion is that the priesthood of Melchizedek endures beyond that of Levi.

A New Priestly Order

The author now poses a rhetorical question to assert that the appearance of another kind of priest (Jesus Christ) exposes the essential weakness of the old priestly order.

> If therefore perfection were by the Levitical priesthood (for under it the people received the law), what further need was there that another priest should rise after the order of Melchisedec, and not be called after the order of Aaron? For the priesthood being changed, there is made of necessity a change also of the law. For he of whom these things are spoken pertaineth to another tribe, of which no man gave attendance at the altar. For it is evident that

THE SUPERIORITY OF MELCHIZEDEK AS HIGH PRIEST

our Lord sprang out of Judah; of which tribe Moses spake nothing concerning priesthood.

—Hebrews 7:11-14

The old system as a whole could not attain perfection; therefore, the idea of perfection can apply only to Jesus Christ. The Law limited the exercise of priesthood to a certain physical lineage, but the new order represented by Jesus Christ has a different source. It is based on the promise of Psalm 110:4: "The LORD hath sworn, and will not repent, Thou art a priest for ever after the order of Melchizedek."

Jesus did not come from any hereditary priestly line. His ancestor was Judah, a tribe not associated with priesthood in the Mosaic Law. The title our Lord obtained has a confessional ring and harkens to the Davidic statement that comes at the beginning of the writer's key passage: "The LORD said unto my Lord, Sit thou at my right hand, until I make thine enemies thy footstool" (Psalm 110:1).

A Priest Forever

The prominent point the author of Hebrews is making here is that of the annulment of the old priesthood by the new, but the operative phrase is *forever*. Jesus Christ is priest through the power of an indestructible life. His ministry as heavenly High Priest has no temporal limits. Death cannot touch Him, because His resurrection shows that He shares God's life.

> And it is yet far more evident: for that after the similitude of Melchisedec there ariseth another priest. Who is made, not after the law of a carnal commandment, but after the power of an endless life. For he testifieth, Thou art a priest for ever after the order of Melchisedec. For there is verily a disannulling of the commandment going before

for the weakness and unprofitableness thereof. For the law made nothing perfect, but the bringing in of a better hope did; by the which we draw nigh unto God.
—Hebrews 7:15-19

Jesus Christ's accession as eternal High Priest is the basis of a *better* hope because it follows Him into the innermost presence of God. Through His sacrifice, He has opened the way for believers to approach God with confidence as they plead for help and offer their own sacrifice of praise.

The Lord Has Sworn

Jesus Christ's resurrection-life is the power that undergirds His eternal priesthood, but it is God's oath that validates the office. The writer cites Psalm 110:4, leaving out the reference to Melchizedek but including the first part of the verse: "The Lord sware and will not repent." The significance of this oath is indicated by means of comparison. Priests in the old dispensation were not required to take an oath before assuming office, nor did God confirm their status with an oath. By contrast, God speaks an oath directly to Christ, which coincides with Jesus' installation as the eternal High Priest. In this way, God guarantees the unchangeable character of His purpose. An unchanging will establishes, validates and guarantees a permanent office.

And inasmuch as not without an oath he was made priest: (For those priests were made without an oath; but this with an oath by him that said unto him, The Lord sware and will not repent, Thou art a priest for ever after the order of Melchisedec:) By so much was Jesus made a surety of a better testament.
—Hebrews 7:20-22

THE SUPERIORITY OF MELCHIZEDEK AS HIGH PRIEST

The eternal nature of Jesus' office ensures that He is the guarantee of a covenant that is better than the old one, much in the same sense that He introduces a better hope. The main point the author is making here is that an Eternal Priest stands as Guarantor of an eternal covenant that stands forever. He is not only the mediator of a new covenant but also the pledge of its enduring character.

An Eternally Effective Priest

In the next passage, the author stresses the permanent effectiveness of Jesus Christ's priesthood:

> And they truly were many priests, because they were not suffered to continue by reason of death: But this man, because he continueth ever, hath an unchangeable priesthood. Wherefore he is able also to save them to the uttermost that come unto God by him, seeing he ever liveth to make intercession for them.
> —Hebrews 7:23-25

The sense of the comparison in verses 23-24 is enhanced by a neat chiasm:

A: the many have become priests
B: through being prevented by death from remaining (in office)
B: through his remaining forever
A: he holds the priesthood permanently

The enduring nature of Jesus Christ's office, attested by the divine oath, contrasts with the momentary tenure of priestly offices held in the old order. The former is eternal; the latter is mortal. Through the heirs of Aaron, the Israelites had a perpetual, albeit finite, priesthood throughout the generations. This manifold priests in a mortal lineage indicate the incompleteness, imperfection and ineffectiveness of their office. The heavenly High Priest always lives to champion the cause of those who are still running the race of faith and endurance.

A Sinless Priest

> For such an high priest became us, who is holy, harmless, undefiled, separate from sinners, and made higher than the heavens; who needeth not daily, as those high priests, to offer up sacrifice, first for his own sins, and then for the people's: for this he did once, when he offered up himself. For the law maketh men high priests which have infirmity; but the word of the oath, which was since the law, maketh the Son, who is consecrated for evermore.
> —Hebrews 7:26-28

While the first three terms—holy, blameless, undefiled—recall the cultic purity ritual that was required for entry into God's presence, they particularly point out the freedom from defilement that the Law required of priests. Jesus Christ belongs in God's presence without prior cleansing because He is a *sinless* Son. In the old order, fellow sinners set high priests apart for service, but in the new order, God exalts the Son and proclaims Him as High Priest. Jesus Christ serves in God's presence by virtue of His personal attributes and appointment. His priestly service does not involve sacrifice, and whereas the earthly high priests had to offer continual sacrifices for others and themselves, the heavenly High Priest offers Himself in one unique and unrepeatable sacrifice. This theology of the Law versus promise in Hebrews runs parallel to Pauline thought: The promise supersedes the Law, because the Law is temporal

THE SUPERIORITY OF MELCHIZEDEK AS HIGH PRIEST

while the promise is eternal. Paul sees Law as moral requirement; Hebrews speaks of Law in terms of cultic regulations. Paul sees God's promise to Abraham as being fulfilled in the righteousness that comes by faith in Christ; Hebrews sees the promise of Psalm 110:4 as being fulfilled in Jesus Christ's eternal priesthood.

Application

No one can add to what Jesus Christ has done to save us. Moreover, Jesus is with the Father as a sign that we have forgiveness of our past, present and future sins. As our High Priest, Jesus Christ is our advocate, the mediator between God and us. He looks after our interests and intercedes for us with God. The Old Testament high priest went before God once a year to plead for the forgiveness of the nation's sins, but Jesus Christ makes perpetual intercession before God for us. Jesus Christ's continuous presence in heaven with the Father assures us that He paid for our sins and that we have forgiveness of sins.

HEBREWS VIII

THE PERFECT SACRIFICE OF THE HEAVENLY HIGH PRIEST

Christ as Minister of a Heavenly Sanctuary

IN THE NEXT passage, the author explains how one who is a heavenly High Priest can offer a sacrifice. This naturally leads to the question of covenant, because covenant, cult and blood are all closely connected.

> Now of the things which we have spoken this is the sum: We have such an high priest, who is set on the right hand of the thrown of the Majesty in the heavens; a minister of the sanctuary, and of the true tabernacle, which the Lord pitched, and not man. For every high priest is ordained to offer gifts and sacrifices: wherefore it is of necessity that this man have somewhat also to offer. For if he were on earth, he should not be a priest, seeing that there are priests that offer gifts according to the law: Who serve unto the example and shadow of heavenly things, as Moses was admonished of God when he was about to make the tabernacle: for, See, saith he, that thou make all things according to the pattern shown to thee in the mount. But

now hath he obtained a more excellent ministry, by how much also he is the mediator of a better covenant, which was established upon better promises.
—Hebrews 8:1-6

The author makes his argument concerning the heavenly High Priest's sanctuary and sacrifice in such a way that the statements about the true sanctuary frame the statements about priestly offerings. Christ is now the heavenly High Priest at God's right hand. Formulated as a confession, this truth recalls the present intercessory office of Jesus Christ.

Two aspects of the high priestly office—sanctuary and sacrifice—reveal the special nature of Christ's office as Minister. Jesus Christ functions in a sanctuary not made by human hands, but in the true tabernacle set up by God. "True" denotes that it is eternally valid, as opposed to that which is temporary. The heavenly sanctuary constituted by the divine presence is not temporary, like the tabernacle in the wilderness, but is eternal. The writer then returns to his prior argument that the old regulations governing priesthood do not apply in the case of the heavenly High Priest. By definition, a heavenly High Priest serves in a heavenly sanctuary.

The author next recalls how God gave Moses specific instructions to build the tabernacle according to the pattern revealed to him on Mount Sinai. The plan that Moses received reflected the form of the original, heavenly sanctuary. The difference between the two sanctuaries underscores the superiority of Jesus Christ's ministry. Moses was the mediator of the old covenant at Mount Sinai; Jesus Christ is a mediator of a better covenant, which does not depend on legal requirement but on better promises. What is essentially a word promise is seen as a word of reproach.

THE PERFECT SACRIFICE OF THE HEAVENLY HIGH PRIEST

The breaking of the Mount Sinai covenant by the Israelites required a new initiative by God.

The Inauguration of a New Covenant

> For if that first covenant had been faultless, then should no place have been sought for the second. For finding fault with them, he saith, Behold, the days come, saith the Lord, when I will make a new covenant with the house of Israel and with the house of Judah: Not according to the covenant that I made with their fathers in the day when I took them by the hand to lead them out of the land of Egypt; because they continued not in my covenant, and I regarded them not, saith the Lord. For this is the covenant that I will make with the house of Israel after those days, saith the Lord; I will put my laws into their mind, and write them in their hearts: and I will be to them a God, and they shall be to me a people: And they shall not teach every man his neighbour, and every man his brother, saying, Know the Lord: for all shall know me, from the least to the greatest. For I will be merciful to their unrighteousness, and their sins and their iniquities will I remember no more. In that he saith, A new covenant, he hath made the first old. Now that which decayeth and waxeth old is ready to vanish away.
> —Hebrews 8:7-13

In using the phrase "I will establish," the author reminds the reader that every covenant (with Noah, Abraham, Israel and David) was made on divine initiative and grace. The first covenant was a sign of God's continuing care of a people whom He rescued from the slavery in Egypt and guided during their desert pilgrimage. The writer lets the text speak for itself: The forefathers did not keep the conditions of the covenant. Disobedience meant the loss of God's extraordinary care. The sins of Israel revealed the weakness of the first covenant and the need for one that was entirely new.

Application

At one time, the prophets had to complain that there was "no knowledge of God in the land":

> Hear the word of the LORD, ye children of Israel: for the LORD hath a controversy with the inhabitants of the land, because there is no truth, nor mercy, nor knowledge of God in the land. . . . My people are destroyed for lack of knowledge: because thou hast rejected knowledge, I will also reject thee, that thou shalt be no priest to me: seeing thou hast forgotten the law of thy God, I will also forget thy children.
> —Hosea 4:1,6

However, as a result of God's new intervention, the goal of the first covenant will be achieved. A faithful God will again have a faithful people. Everybody will know God, which obviates the need for special instruction.

The essential mark of the new covenant is the complete removal of sin. In mercy, God both forgives and forgets. Note also that in verse 12 the author stresses, "For the priesthood being changed, there is made of necessity a change also of the law." This is important for the writer, and he cites it as a separate word of the Spirit at the conclusion of his discourse on Jesus Christ's high-priestly work. By mentioning a new covenant, God declares the first one obsolete.

HEBREWS IX

THE EARTHLY SANCTUARY'S APPOINTMENTS

The Tabernacle

> Then verily the first covenant had also ordinances of divine service, and a worldly sanctuary. For there was a tabernacle made; the first, wherein was the candlestick, and the table, and the showbread; which is called the sanctuary. And after the second veil, the tabernacle which is called the Holiest of all; which had the golden censer, and the ark of the covenant overlaid round about with gold, wherein was the golden pot that had manna, and Aaron's rod that budded, and the tables of the covenant; and over it the cherubims of glory shadowing the mercy seat; of which we cannot now speak particularly.
> —Hebrews 9:1-5

THE TABERNACLE WAS a double tent set within a court. The outer compartment, entered through a first curtain, was called the Holy Place. On its south side stood the lamp stand, or menorah, made of pure gold, with three branches rising on each side of the main stem, forming seven candleholders. On the north side stood a table made of acacia wood and overlaid with gold. The bread of the presence was placed on it, which was bread set before the presence of God, as well as certain sacrificial utensils. Each Sabbath, 12 freshly baked cakes were placed on the table to serve as standing cereal offering. Only the priests were permitted to eat this holy bread.

A second curtain led to the inner sanctuary, the Holy of Holies. The description of its contents is problematic, as the golden altar of incense was not originally located on the second tent, but the first tent. The simplest explanation is that the author is referring to a later positioning of the altar of incense in the Holy of Holies. However, the inner sanctuary could never be entered without incense from this altar. The authors concern is to link the altar with the Ark of the Covenant; blood was sprinkled on both on the Day of Atonement. The principal object in the inner shrine was the Ark of the Covenant, a box of acacia wood overlaid with gold. Also called the Ark of the Testimony, it contained the two tablets of stone as a lasting witness to God's covenant will.

The author places special significance on the mercy seat or place of atonement because it was sprinkled with blood by the high priest on the Day of Atonement. He saw it as the earthly counterpart of God's heavenly throne. It represented the earthly presence of God who is elsewhere described as the enthronement on the cherubim. Jesus Christ's enthronement now occupies the mercy seat.

The Priestly Ritual

> Now when these things were thus ordained, the priests went always into the first tabernacle, accomplishing the service of God. But into the second went the high priest

THE EARTHLY SANCTUARY'S APPOINTMENTS

alone once every year, not without blood, which he offered for himself, and for the errors of the people: The Holy Ghost this signifying, that the way into the holiest of all was not yet made manifest, while as the first tabernacle was yet standing: Which was a figure for the time then present, in which were offered both gifts and sacrifices, that could not make him that did the service perfect, as pertaining to the conscience; which stood only in the meats and drinks, and divers washings, and carnal ordinances, imposed on them until the time of reformation.

—Hebrews 9:6-10

According to Hebrews 9:6-10, ordinary priests had the outer tabernacle as their domain. Only the high priest was allowed to enter the inner sanctuary, and he could do this only once each year on Yom Kippur. Unlawful entry into the inner sanctuary carried the death penalty. The high priest could enter only if he was bearing blood to remove the defilement of the people's sin. Clothed in special regalia, he entered the Holy of Holies twice, once to sprinkle the mercy seat with the blood of a bull sacrificed for himself and his household, and a second time to sprinkle the blood of a goat sacrificed for the people. This was followed by the ritual of a scapegoat being driven into the wilderness, bearing the sins of the people.

The writer of Hebrews sees a deeper meaning in these regulations: they point to their inadequacy. The annual entry of the high priest into the inner sanctuary was an exception to the general rule. The way to the sanctuary was not disclosed, because there was no open access for all into the heavenly sanctuary, of which the earthly Holy of Holies was merely a symbol. Only Jesus Christ opens up access into the true sanctuary of God's eternal presence.

The old system could not breach the gap between sinful humanity and God because it offered only an outward ceremonial purification. The Law made nothing perfect, so the rites it provided could not perfectly cleanse the peoples' conscience. The constant repetition of these rites could not remove the peoples' inner awareness that sin separated them from a holy God, and this awareness reached into the heart and mind. In particular, it was the duty of the high priest to bathe himself after the ritual of Yom Kippur. This was a temporary demand by God until the establishment of a new and perfect order of worship in which consciences are perfectly cleansed.

Eternal Redemption Secured by Blood

> But Christ being come an high priest of good things to come, by a greater and more perfect tabernacle, not made with hands, that is to say, not of this building; neither by the blood of goats and calves, but by his own blood he entered in once into the holy place, having obtained eternal redemption for us. For if the blood of bulls and of goats, and the ashes of an heifer sprinkling the unclean, sanctifieth to the purifying of the flesh: How much more shall the blood of Christ, who through the eternal Spirit offered himself without spot to God, purge your conscience from dead works to serve the living God?
> —Hebrews 9:11-14

The author states that the better things to which the Law pointed have arrived with the appearance of Jesus Christ. His entry into the heavenly sanctuary is part of His exaltation. This even presupposes His sacrificial death. The exalted Christ is recognized as the heavenly High Priest on the basis of His death as a unique and effective sacrifice.

THE EARTHLY SANCTUARY'S APPOINTMENTS

Using the analogy of the earthly high priest, the writer states that Christ passed through the greater and perfect tent before entering the heavenly Holy of Holies. The writer views the heavens, which Jesus Christ passed all the way through, as the equivalent of the tabernacle's first chamber, the Holy Place. He distinguishes between the created heavens that will pass away and the heavens that represent the transcendent realm of God.

Access to God is possible only through the medium of blood. Jesus Christ's entry into the heavenly sanctuary by means of His own blood denotes more than the completion of a perfect sacrifice and more than the ratification of His death as a saving event. The Levitical priests entered the earthly inner sanctuary once each year; Jesus entered the heavenly sanctuary once for all. In the old cult, animal blood was sprinkled on people to remove ceremonial defilement; the blood of Jesus Christ is more potent than that of animals and purifies the conscience by removing the guilt of sin. There are two reasons for the absolute effectiveness of Jesus Christ's self-sacrifice: (1) He was without the blemish of sin, and (2) His sacrifice is possible through everlasting Spirit. The life-giving Spirit stands in contrast to flesh as mortal.

A New Covenant Inaugurated in Blood

The author of Hebrews will now use a legal argument to remind his readers that the validity of a human will rests with the person making the testament, but it will come into force only after his or her death. The focal point now moves to Christ's death as being one that establishes a covenant that is qualitatively different. Beneath the old covenant there was temporary and external cleansing through repeated sacrifices. In the new covenant, there is permanent emancipation from sin.

> And for this cause he is the mediator of the new testament, that by means of death, for the redemption of the transgressions that were under the first testament, they which are called might receive the promise of eternal inheritance. For where a testament is, there must also of necessity be the death of the testator. For a testament is of force after men are dead: otherwise it is of no strength at all while the testator liveth. Whereupon neither the first testament was dedicated without blood. For when Moses had spoken every precept to all the people according to the law, he took the blood of calves and of goats, with water, and scarlet wool, and hyssop, and sprinkled both the book, and all the people, saying, This is the blood of the testament which God hath enjoined unto you. Moreover he sprinkled with blood both the tabernacle, and all the vessels of the ministry. And almost all things are by the law purged with blood; and without shedding of blood is no remission.
> —Hebrews 9:15-22

A sacrifice with eternal power gives an everlasting inheritance and fulfills God's promise of complete forgiveness from all sins. The inheritance is a gift to those who, like the Israelites in the wilderness, are called to follow a path leading to a promise. This promise is guaranteed to all siblings of the Son, who is the heir of all things. Elements of Hebrews 9:19 that are not taken from the Exodus account draw attention to the action of sprinkling. Scarlet wool, hyssop and water were used in rites for the purification of lepers and in the rites of priests officiating at the sacrifice of the red heifer. The hyssop was also used to sprinkle the blood of the Passover lamb in Egypt. The author mentions goat blood because it belongs to the ritual of Yom Kippur.

Additional elements add to the idea that the Mosaic covenant was inaugurated with comprehensive sprinkling.

THE EARTHLY SANCTUARY'S APPOINTMENTS

Moses smeared and sprinkled blood on and around the altar at the consecration of Aaron and his sons to the priesthood. Note in verse 22 that the author states that all the people and every vessel were consecrated by sprinkling. The writer was thinking here of the power of Jesus Christ's blood, as he stresses that the blood of animals was able to produce only an external cleansing. Perfect redemption is provided only through the blood of Jesus Christ.

A Completely Effective Sacrifice

> It was therefore necessary that the patterns of things in the heavens should be purified with these; but the heavenly things themselves with better sacrifices than these. For Christ is not entered into the holy places made with hands, which are the figures of the true; but into heaven itself, now to appear in the presence of God for us: Nor yet that he should offer himself often, as the high priest entereth into the holy place every year with blood of others; for then must he often have suffered since the foundation of the world: but now once in the end of the world hath he appeared to put away sin by the sacrifice of himself. And as it is appointed unto men once to die, but after this the judgment: So Christ was once offered to bear the sins of many: and unto them that look for him shall he appear the second time without sin unto salvation.
>
> —Hebrews 9:23-28

The author returns to the typology of Yom Kippur and to the analogy between the actions of the high priests and those of Christ. Jesus, who enters the heavenly sanctuary at His exaltation, now continues to appear before God to advocate on our behalf. Through Him, others can now appear before God. Thus, there is no need for an earthly temple, for a mediating priesthood, or for continuing sacrifices. Jesus

Christ supersedes all these through His self-sacrificial death and in the offering of His blood in the heavenly sanctuary. The annual rite of carrying animal blood into the Holy of Holies no longer has any relevance. Christ's sacrifice is once and for all, and therefore eternally effective.

Application

Animal sacrifice had to occur repeatedly, but the sacrifice of Christ was eternal. Jesus Christ will appear again, not to be judged but to judge, and not to deal with sin but to save those who call upon Him. He will make a second and final appearance to vindicate the faith of believers and to call to their eternal rest those who are eagerly waiting for Him. This consummation will be the final proof of His effective sacrifice. Jesus Christ's sacrifice transforms our lives and hearts and makes us clean on the inside. His sacrifice is infinitely more effective than animal sacrifice.

HEBREWS X

THE SACRIFICES UNDER THE LAW WERE INEFFECTIVE

The Law Is a Pale Reflection of God's Will

> For the law having a shadow of good things to come, and not the very image of the things, can never with those sacrifices which they offered year by year continually make the comers thereunto perfect. For then would they not have ceased to be offered? Because that the worshippers once purged should have had no more conscience of sins. But in those sacrifices there is a remembrance again made of sins every year. For it is not possible that the blood of bulls and of goats should take away sins.
> —Hebrews 10:1-4

REVELATION IN JESUS Christ shows that the Law was never intended to be anything but a pale reflection of God's final will. In support of reasons already stated, the author says that the annual ritual of Yom Kippur could not perfect worshipers. It could not remove the guilt that stains the conscience and bars sinners from God's holy presence.

The old sacrificial system served a purpose in the divine plan through its ability to offer more than external cleansing. Annual sacrifices and application of animal blood served as a reminder to the people that sin is not permanently dealt with. This particular level of spiritual deficiency was unavoidable, as the people's knowledge of God and forgiveness of sin were surrounded with sacrificial cults. Material method cannot remove moral defilement. The spiritual significance of sacrificial ritual might have shown a material foreshadowing or article of lesson of a moral and spiritual truth. This action prophetically points to the perfect cleansing effected by the blood of Jesus Christ.

Christ Has Effectively Obeyed God's Will

> Wherefore when he cometh into the world, he saith, Sacrifice and offering thou wouldest not, but a body hast thou prepared me: In burnt offerings and sacrifices for sin thou hast had no pleasure. Then said I, Lo, I come (in the volume of the book it is written of me,) to do thy will, O God. Above when he said, sacrifice and offering and burnt offerings and offering for sin thou wouldest not, neither hadst pleasure therein; which are offered by the law; then said he, Lo, I come to do thy will, O God. He taketh away the first, that he may establish the second. By the which will we are sanctified through the offering of the body of Jesus Christ once for all.
> —Hebrews 10:5-10

In the gospel tradition, Jesus cites Hosea 6:6—"For I desired mercy, and not sacrifice; and the knowledge of God more than burnt offerings"—to call for true inner obedience rather than performance of external ceremonies (see Matt. 9:13). All past sacrifices are superseded by Jesus Christ's obedience in offering His own body. The perfect self-sacrifice

THE SACRIFICES UNDER THE LAW WERE INEFFECTIVE

of Jesus Christ fulfilled and transcended the spiritual principles that underlay these different types of sacrifice. It was while He was in His body of flesh and blood that the Son learned obedience through suffering in order to sanctify sinners. The author's contrast is not between sacrifice and obedience but between the involuntary sacrifice of ordinary animals and sacrifice through obedience—the sacrifice of a coherent and Spiritual Man. The prophetic word points to Jesus Christ as an obedient Son.

The author's brief midrash treatment in verses 5-9 focuses on Christ's holiness as the means by which God's final will is effected. Under the prerequisite of the new covenant is the stipulation that God's law shall henceforth be embossed in the hearts of His people. It was extremely appropriate that this should be most true of the One who ratified the new covenant through His obedience and blood. The verses the author cites (Psalm 40:6-8) read as a programmatic declaration of God's lack of pleasure in the sacrifices under the Law. The author concludes that Jesus Christ came to do God's will by offering Himself as a sacrifice.

A final exegetical statement in verses 8-10 picks up two key verses from the previous quotation in Psalm 40:6-8. Jesus affirms God's determination in offering His own body as a sacrifice. The final significance of this event for the community of believers is expressed as a confession. The latter denotes that radical cleansing from sin which, after providing access to God, is the basis for doing of God's will in life through worship, including spoken praise and obedience.

By the obedience of one shall many be made righteous (see Romans 5:19), to the extent that He "sanctified" His people and granted the "perfection" that was not possible under the old system of sacrifices. Jesus Christ as the fulfillment of God's will to the extreme involved the "offering" once and for all of His body. The Incarnation took place so that the sin of the whole world could be taken away by the offering of His body. That is why sanctification and access into the presence of God were made obtainable through the offering of Christ's body.

Whether the author speaks of Christ's body or His blood, it is His incarnate life that He yielded to God in obedience until His death. Jesus Christ's presentation of His life to God was a perfect sacrifice; thus there is no need to repeat it. The significance of the sanctification received by those who accept Him is their inward cleansing from sin, and they are transformed to be suitable for the presence of God—to present Him satisfactory worship. The sanctifying will of God was made possible by a human being who is now the heavenly King.

Christ's Exaltation Shows the Finality of His Sacrifice

> And every priest standeth daily ministering and offering oftentimes the same sacrifices, which can never take away sins: But this man, after he had offered one sacrifice for sins for ever, sat down on the right hand of God; from henceforth expecting till his enemies be made his footstool. For by one offering he hath perfected for ever them that are sanctified.
> —Hebrews 10:11-14

The priests must carry out their tasks repeatedly, which is an indication of the incompleteness of these tasks. In contrast to multiple repeated, yet ineffective, sacrifices, Christ offers a single sacrifice once and for all that effectively removes sins. Because He sits at the right hand of God and has progressed through the act of atonement to exaltation, His sacrifice is complete, final and completely effective.

THE SACRIFICES UNDER THE LAW WERE INEFFECTIVE

The Aaronic priests stood throughout the performance of their sacred service in the sanctuary—they never sat down. The author notes that their sacred duties were never completed; hence the need for them to repeat the sacrifices. Whether this repetition was done on a daily basis or annually, the point is that repetition of these sacrifices was necessary, though none of them could eradicate sin or effectively cleanse a person's conscience on a permanent basis. The completion of one sacrifice signified that a related sacrifice would be offered soon after—and that this would go on forever. This is the reason why the ancient priests never sat down in God's presence when they presented a sacrifice to Him.

In keeping with the perfection of Jesus Christ's self-sacrifice when He had presented it to God, He sat down. There was no need for further sacrificial service by the High Priest who appeared on earth in the fullness of time to lay away sin and sanctify His people once for all. The guarantee of a completed work and sacrifice was a seated High Priest.

The heavenly High Priest has a continual ministry to fulfill on behalf of His people as He sits at the right hand of the heavenly Father. This is the ministry of intercession based on the sacrifice presented and accepted once and for all, but not the regular or continual offering of His sacrifice. The fact that Jesus Christ is seated is a symbol that His sacrificial work is completed, but the author highlights the value of His sacrifice and the dignity of His personality by indicating that He has taken His seat not simply in the *presence* of God but also at the *right hand* of God. Christ has been exalted to the place of highest glory from the humiliation of the cross. Therefore, His people, with confidence, may avail themselves of High Priestly aid with the assurance that they have direct access to all the grace and power of

God. In Hebrews 10:13, the author cites Psalm 110:1 to show that Jesus Christ is no longer a sacrificing priest but a reigning king. His statement describes the effects of Christ completing His work: He Himself has been perfected in His elevation to God's right hand, and God has brought Him to His final goal. The author also makes an implied warning here that his readers must avoid being numbered among the enemies of the exalted Jesus Christ and instead become His friends and companions by persevering in their devotion until the end.

He who was perfected can now perfect sinners; He brings them to their heavenly goal. Jesus Christ by His self-oblation (solemn offering to God) accomplished once and for all what generations of Levitical sacrifices had failed to achieve. The attainment of the objective of those sacrifices after hundreds of years was impossible.

Most early converts to Christianity (both Jews and Gentiles) had been used to a particular type of worship in which animal sacrifices played a major role. That there was no place for such sacrifices in the new method of worship was a tribute to the fact that the death of Jesus Christ had forever rendered them obsolete. The logic of this argument was implicit in these converts' most elementary understanding of the gospel. The self-sacrifice of Jesus Christ removed the impurities of moral corruption and transgression in His people and assured them of everlasting preservation in a right standing with God. From this, we see that the exceptional effects of the sacrifice of Jesus Christ are that through it, (1) the consciences of His people are cleansed from guilt; (2) they have confidence to approach the presence of God as accepted worshipers; and (3) they can be brought into faultless relation to God and experience the fulfillment of the earlier promise of the old covenant.

THE SACRIFICES UNDER THE LAW WERE INEFFECTIVE

The New Covenant Brings Effective Forgiveness

> Whereof the Holy Ghost also is a witness to us: for after that he had said before, This is the covenant that I will make with them after those days, saith the Lord, I will put my laws into their hearts, and in their minds will I write them; and their sins and iniquities will I remember no more. Now where remission of these is, there is no more offering for sin.
> —Hebrews 10:15-18

The abridged quotation the author uses here from Jeremiah 31:33 places the writing of God's will in the hearts and minds of people in close proximity to His "forgetting" of their sins. Those who are sanctified are able to do the will of God from a willingness that arises from their hearts. Such obedience is possible because God does not remember their sins; the effective sacrifice of Christ blots them out of God's memory forever.

Complete removal of sin through Christ's sacrifice means that there is no longer the necessity of any further offering for sin. The writer thus dwells on the unity of divine will between Jesus and God. The verses he cites from Psalm 40:6-8 and Jeremiah 31:33 are linked because Jesus, who mediates the new covenant, embodies one of its essential features: inner obedience.

> Sacrifice and offering thou didst not desire; mine ears hast thou opened: burnt offering and sin offering hast thou not required. Then said I, Lo, I come: in the volume of the book it is written of me. I delight to do thy will, O my God: yea, thy law is within my heart.
> —Psalm 40:6-8

> But this shall be the covenant that I will make with the house of Israel; After those days, saith the Lord, I will put

> my law in their inward parts, and write it in their hearts; and will be their God, and they shall be my people. And they shall teach no more every man his neighbour, and every man his brother, saying, Know the Lord: for they shall all know me, from the least of them unto the greatest of them, saith the LORD: for I will forgive their iniquity, and I will remember their sin no more.
> —Jeremiah 31:33-34

The fact that Christ completes God's will in offering Himself makes it possible for the people of the new covenant to do God's will.

Hold Your Confession and Draw Near to God

> Having therefore, brethren, boldness to enter into the holiest by the blood of Jesus, by a new and living way, which he hath consecrated for us, through the veil, that is to say, his flesh; and having an high priest over the house of God; Let us draw near with a true heart in full assurance of faith, having our hearts sprinkled from an evil conscience, and our bodies washed with pure water. Let us hold fast the profession of our faith without wavering; (for he is faithful that promised;) and let us consider one another to provoke unto love and to good works: Not forsaking the assembling of ourselves together, as the manner of some is; but exhorting one another: and so much the more, as ye see the day approaching.
> —Hebrews 10:19-25

The writer's exposition now gives way to personal exhortation through key arguments about the absolute superiority of Christ as Son and High Priest, His perfect sacrifice, and the certainty we can have of salvation in Him. The following terms reappear: "sanctuary," "priest," "approach," "sprinkle," "conscience," "confession" and

THE SACRIFICES UNDER THE LAW WERE INEFFECTIVE

"promise." The author's fundamental statement is highly structured and followed by a series of three appeals that center on faith, hope and love.

Two Affirmations. Direct address and appeals in the all-encompassing first-person plural in verses 19-21 are features of the author's parenetic style. He states that while there were restrictions that circumvented the privilege of symbolic entry into God's presence in earthly Israel's sanctuary, believers in Jesus Christ have a "boldness" that enables them to enter the heavenly sanctuary through Him. In the earthly sanctuary, only the high priest could exercise this privilege at a specific time and under certain conditions, but now believers can confidently enter God's sanctuary by means of the blood of Jesus Christ. The author of Hebrews urges his readers to avail themselves of the opportunity to be cleansed within, consecrated and made perfect by the sacrifice of Jesus Christ to enjoy the sovereignty of access into the holy presence of God.

The author gives a further assurance that the same means by which the high priest entered into God's presence will continue to be open for His people to follow Him to the Father. According to this passage, "through the veil" believers in Jesus Christ have free entrance into the very throne of God. He alone opens up the way through the curtain through His flesh. His blood made entry possible in a double sense: He first opened up the way with the offering of His blood, and now He makes it possible for others to enter by the application of that cleansing, life-giving blood. The fact that Jesus Christ fulfils His ministry as "a great High Priest over the house of God" should enhance the confidence of His people in entering God's presence.

Three Appeals. The author's first appeal, "let us draw near" (10:22), echoes his words in 4:16 and invites the readers to avail themselves of priestly access to God's presence based on the past actions and present function of the heavenly High Priest. The author of Hebrews repeats this phrase to emphasize that there are now no conditions to enter into God's presence as there were in times of old when the high priest could only make an annual access into the Holy of Holies on the Day of Atonement. The author elaborates that those who experienced the inward cleansing brought about by Jesus Christ's self-suffering may be marked by sincerity of heart and "full assurance of faith."

It is obvious that the "sprinkling of the heart" denotes an inward, spiritual cleansing. The author of Hebrews previously noted that under the new order, the counterpart of the old ritual cleansing is the "water for impurity" (see Hebrew 9:13). Individuals who are bold enough to enter the heavenly refuge through the blood of Jesus Christ are purified by that same blood and are able to stand in the divine presence of God. It is the cleansing of their conscience that purges the barricade that previously prevented their free entrance. In this sense, the author may be referring to the requirement that on the Day of Atonement, the priest had to wash his body in water (see Leviticus 16:4) before putting on the linen garment to approach God in the Holy of Holies. The present reality is that Christian baptism does not merely consist of outward application of water; that outward application is the noticeable sign of inward and spiritual cleansing shaped by the power of God in individuals that come to Him through Jesus Christ. Water baptism is not intended to remove bodily impurity but, according to 1 Peter 3:21, to serve as "the answer of a good conscience toward God."

The author's second appeal is "Let us hold fast the profession of our faith without wavering" (10:23). Approaching God in worship requires a true heart—one that is genuine and sincere—for only the pure in heart can stand in God's

THE SACRIFICES UNDER THE LAW WERE INEFFECTIVE

holy presence. It requires the full assurance of faith that clings to the certainty that what God promises is true. Bodies washed with pure water are a parallel expression for the present effects of Jesus Christ's saving death. The application of water and blood marked the inauguration of the old covenant, but the new "cleansing by blood and water" confirms the reality of the new covenant. For the believer, faithfully clinging to the certainty of God's promises will ensure that present or future trials can be endured without wavering.

A call to communal expression of love in 10:24-25 completes the authors' series of appeals. Good deeds accompany a life of worship and will reinforce the fact that the readers have been cleansed from dead works. They have been told to consider Jesus Christ, to fix their eyes on Him as their hope, and now they are to consider one another so that the house of God remains a family of love. The readers need to stimulate one another to "love and good works," thus ensuring this will happen. The author warns that if they stay away from one another, this will never come to pass; consequently, they must welcome every chance to come together for a common purpose and enjoy their fellowship in faith and hope.

There is evidence here that some members of the community were being slack in corporately expressing faith, hope and love by neglecting to meet together for communal worship. The author has evidently observed that some were withdrawing from Christian fellowship, and it is for this reason that he exhorts his readers to continue meeting together on a regular basis. In Romans 15:7, Paul also urged the Roman Christians to welcome and receive one another for the glory of God as Jesus Christ welcomed and received them. From this, we are made to understand that toward the end of the apostolic age, there was a tendency by some individuals to withdraw from the Christian fellowship. Levity, lethargy and fatigue were, at times, enough to disconnect a person from the society. In addition, many were induced to withdraw from Christian fellowship and from the regular worship by a narcissistic sense of supremacy—they believed that they were able to dispense with the religious support of the general public. A number of other people turned away from attending public worship because they feared the authorities would recognize them as Christians.

Do Not Spurn Christ's Sacrifice

> For if we sin willfully after that we have received the knowledge of the truth, there remaineth no more sacrifice for sins, but a certain fearful looking for of judgment and fiery indignation, which shall devour the adversaries. He that despised Moses' law died without mercy under two or three witnesses: Of how much sorer punishment, suppose ye, shall he be thought worthy, who hath trodden under foot the Son of God, and hath counted the blood of the covenant, wherewith he was sanctified, an unholy thing, and hath done despite unto the Spirit of grace? For we know him that hath said, Vengeance belongeth unto me, I will recompense, saith the Lord. And again, The Lord shall judge his people. It is a fearful thing to fall into the hands of the living God.
> —Hebrews 10:26-31

The appeals the author makes in Hebrews 10:19-25 is based on the thesis that there is no longer any offering for sin in view of Christ's sacrifice. His warning against apostasy is couched in vivid language, and he uses biblical references to underline the solemn lesson that curses, not blessing, must fall on those who reject God's covenant. The

THE SACRIFICES UNDER THE LAW WERE INEFFECTIVE

author's opening statement in 10:26 points to the terrible consequences of a final rejection of Christ.

This passage was destined to have repercussions in Christian history much further than what the author could have foreseen. By "sin willfully," he means sinning in a way for which the Old Testament law of atonement did not make available any forgiveness. The author repeats the argument that despising the saving message spoken by the Son of God brings penalties that are more severe than the sanctions affixed to the Law of Moses. The author has pointed out more than once that in Jesus Christ, Christians have a High Priest who can succor them when they are tempted, have compassion for them in their infirmities, and bear gently with them when they wander away from the pursuit of righteousness through lack of knowledge. Those who neglect worship gatherings run a terrible risk, for neglect can become contempt, leading to a final stance in which they willfully persist in sin.

In this sense, the writer is referring to a person's deliberate rejection of the gospel after conversion. Those who turn away from the living God in apostasy reject the sacrifice for sins provided by Christ, thus negating His saving power. His sacrifice is no longer valid for them because they have contemptuously rejected the basis of salvation and can therefore no longer be restored to repentance. Note that when the author uses language like this, he chooses his words with caution. To spurn the Son of God—to trample Him underfoot—signifies disdain of the highest order. Through the covenant blood of Jesus Christ, He sanctified, cleansed and brought His people to God. To ascribe His sacrifice as no better than a common death (see Acts 21:28) is to repudiate both the sacrifice and all the blessings that flow from it, outraging the Spirit of mercy (see Zechariah 12:10). In Mark 3:29, Jesus said that such a person is "guilty of an eternal damnation." According to Deuteronomy 13:8 and 19:13, these people were not to be pitied. Under Israel's covenant law, anyone who was convicted based on adequate testimony of a purposeful breach was liable up to the death penalty. Under the new order, the spiritual death that lies in store for the apostate is a much greater punishment than the penalty of physical death.

Those who consciously distance themselves from the source of Christ's holiness become *contaminated* by His holiness. The author has a profound conviction of the awesome holiness of the Divine Majesty, and while he uses these fearful words repeatedly as a warning to the ungodly of the dangers that lie ahead for them if they do not change their ways, his main application is to the community of God. The prophet Isaiah made a similar statement after God had acted so powerfully on behalf of His people by removing the Assyrian threat from Jerusalem: "Who among us shall dwell with the devouring fire? Who among us shall dwell with everlasting burnings?" (Isaiah 33:14). During that judgment period, Israel discovered new thing about the nature of God who dwell in their mist continually through the revelation of the consuming righteousness of God which they just witness spoke vociferously to them than its effect on Sennacherib's warriors who plummet before it.

Deuteronomy 17:2-7 stipulates that any person guilty of transgressing God's covenant by idolatry should be put to death:

> If there be found among you, within any of thy gates which the Lord thy God giveth thee, man or woman, that hath wrought wickedness in the sight of the Lord thy God, in transgressing his covenant, and hath gone and served other gods, and worshipped them, either the sun, or moon, or any of the host of heaven, which

THE SACRIFICES UNDER THE LAW WERE INEFFECTIVE

> I have not commanded: And it be told thee, and thou hast heard of it, and inquired diligently, and, behold, it be true, and the thing certain, that such abomination is wrought in Israel: Then shalt thou bring forth that man or that woman, which have committed that wicked thing, unto thy gates, even that man or that woman, and shalt stone them with stones, till they die. At the mouth of two witnesses, or three witnesses, shall he that is worthy of death be put to death; but at the mouth of one witness he shall not be put to death. The hands of the witnesses shall be first upon him to put him to death, and afterward the hands of all the people. So thou shalt put the evil away from among you.
> —Deuteronomy 17:2-7

Christians know that God is the one who saves, but He cannot be expected to turn a blind eye toward willful disobedience. In the writer's view, apostasy is no better than idolatry. This does not imply that his readers are looking for security in other gods; the grim warning against apostasy simply suggests that the author sees a potentially disastrous situation in the community. His pastoral insight sees beyond the present to final eventualities, so he designs his rhetoric to shock the audience out of its present complacency.

Endurance Will Gain the Promised Reward

> But call to remembrance the former days, in which, after ye were illuminated, ye endured a great fight of afflictions; partly, whilst ye were made a gazingstock both by reproaches and afflictions; and partly, whilst ye became companions of them that were so used. For ye had compassion of me in my bonds, and took joyfully the spoiling of your goods, knowing in yourselves that ye have in heaven a better and an enduring substance. Cast not away therefore your confidence, which hath great recompence

of reward. For ye have need of patience, that, after ye have done the will of God, ye might receive the promise. For yet a little while, and he that shall come will come, and will not tarry. Now the just shall live by faith: but if any man draw back, my soul shall have no pleasure in him. But we are not of them who draw back unto perdition; but of them that believe to the saving of the soul."
—Hebrews 10:32-39

Presumably, the readers' crises of suffering took place shortly after they had been enlightened in the process of conversion. Paul linked the Christian contest with suffering, and this aspect is dominant in the author's use of the athletic metaphor in Hebrews. The use of this metaphor as a standard picture for Christian martyrdom begins with the portrayal of Peter and Paul as athletes for Christ. Four statements in Hebrews 10:33-34 recall that the believers' persecution involved verbal and physical attacks. To be publicly exposed means, literally, to be placed on public show, as in a theater. The author does not dishearten his readers, but encourages them to emerge triumphant from the present test of their faith. He reminds them of how they withstood a severe trial in the earlier days of their lives as Christians, immediately after their "enlightenment." While the people the author addresses had undergone persecution, none of them had ever suffered martyrdom. Thus, they secured a place for themselves among those whom the Son of Man said, "I was in prison, and ye came unto me" (Matthew 25:36; see also Isaiah 58:7).

The response to this crisis in the community was solidarity. Those who were not made the butt of public humiliation or subjected to violence clearly identified themselves with those who were, as indicated by the language of partnership. This language recalls Christ's solidarity with

THE SACRIFICES UNDER THE LAW WERE INEFFECTIVE

humanity and the picture of Christians as holy partners or sharers in heavenly things.

The author states that the believers' practical expression of solidarity was also seen through their compassion for those in prison. In the ancient world, prisoners had to look to visitors to provide them with proper food and clothing; however, here the writer is more concerned with the community's motivation for their bold confession and group solidarity than with details of their sufferings. Members could cheerfully accept loss of earthly possessions, knowing they have something in heaven that belongs to them.

The author's recollections give way to direct exhortation. He states that confidence is the mark of those who belong to God's household and can boldly approach the divine throne. Endurance is necessary to gain the reward, just as stamina is essential for the athlete. Abraham and others in Israel's history are outstanding examples of faith that endures to receive God's promises, but the final paragon of endurance is Jesus Christ.

A verse from Isaiah 26:20, "Come, my people, enter thou into thy chambers, and shut thy doors about thee: hide thyself as it were for a little moment, until the indignation be overpast," lies behind the author's introductory phrase in verse 37. It is part of a call to retreat to safety for a short time, until God's judgment on Israel's enemies has passed. In verse 38, the author's quotation from Habakkuk 2:4 inverts the two parts of the verse: "the just shall live by his faith" is applied to the Christian believer who is tempted to wonder if Jesus Christ shall come again in accordance with His promise, while the warning about the divine displeasure that will rest upon those who draw back is applied to those who yield to the enticement to relapse from their Christian profession back into their previous method of existence.

Those who persist in faith shall gain their lives, while those who shrink back shall corroborate themselves reprobate.

The fact that the author reproduces this clause simultaneously with part of its context accentuates the onward-looking disposition of saving faith: faith always includes its companion "hope." This calls to mind the words of our Lord Jesus Christ to His disciples when He warned them of coming days that would test their faith severely: "In your patience possess ye your souls" (Luke 21:19). The author desires his readers to demonstrate this type of patience endurance, and he is convinced that because of his solemn warnings they shall certainly demonstrate it and gain true life.

The author then provides an additional assertion of his confidence in his readers, saying, "We are not of them who draw back unto perdition; but of them that believe to the saving of the soul" (Hebrews 10:39). They had begun their Christian profession in that carefree spirit that accepts without questioning Jesus' guarantee in Mark 8:35: "For whosoever will save his life shall lose it; but whosoever shall lose his life for my sake and the gospel's, the same shall save it." The author is stating that if they maintain that spirit of faith to the end, they will surely gain their souls and grasp eternal life. This is the solid assurance of truth as it pertains to the author and his readers alike.

HEBREWS XI

THE FAITH OF THE PATRIARCHS

The Faith of Abraham and the Early Patriarchs

Now faith is the substance of things hoped for, the evidence of things not seen. For by it the elders obtained a good report. Through faith we understand that the worlds were framed by the word of God, so that things which are seen were not made of things which do appear. By faith Abel offered unto God a more excellent sacrifice than Cain, by which he obtained witness that he was righteous, God testifying of his gifts: and by it he being dead yet speaketh. By faith Enoch was translated that he should not see death; and was not found, because God had translated him: for before his translation he had this testimony, that he pleased God. But without faith it is impossible to please him: for he that cometh to God must believe that he is, and that he is a rewarder of them that diligently seek him. By faith Noah, being warned of God of things not seen as yet, moved with fear, prepared an ark to the saving of his house; by the which he condemned the world, and became heir of the righteousness which is by faith. By faith Abraham, when he was called to go out into a place which he should after receive for an inheritance, obeyed; and he went out, not knowing whither he went. By faith he sojourned in the land of promise, as in a strange country, dwelling in tabernacles with Isaac and Jacob, the heirs with him of the same promise: For he looked for a city which hath foundations, whose builder and maker is God. Through faith also Sarah herself received strength to conceive seed, and was delivered of a child when she was past age, because she judged him faithful who had promised. Therefore sprang there even of one, and him as good as dead, so many as the stars of the sky in multitude, and as the sand which is by the sea shore innumerable. These all died in faith, not having received the promises, but having seen them afar off, and were persuaded of them, and embraced them, and confessed that they were strangers and pilgrims on the earth. For they that say such things declare plainly that they seek a country. And truly, if they had been mindful of that country from whence they came out, they might have had opportunity to have returned. But now they desire a better country, that is, an heavenly: wherefore God is not ashamed to be called their God: for he hath prepared for them a city. By faith Abraham, when he was tried, offered up Isaac: and he that had received the promises offered up his only begotten son, of whom it was said, That in Isaac shall thy seed be called: Accounting that God was able to raise him up, even from the dead; from whence also he received him in a figure. By faith Isaac blessed Jacob and Esau concerning things to come. By faith Jacob, when he was a dying, blessed both the sons of Joseph; and worshipped, leaning upon the top of his staff. By faith Joseph, when he died, made mention of the departing of the children of Israel; and gave commandment concerning his bones.

—Hebrews 11:1-22

THE FAITH OF THE PATRIARCHS

TRADITION HELPS TO infer from the biblical record that Abel, Enoch and Noah lived by faith. In the case of Abraham, the writer cites a figure long celebrated as the father of faith. The repetition of the verb "to set out" in Hebrews 11:8 is deliberate: Faith requires a "going out" from earthly securities before it can lead into God's presence and the final rest.

In describing the patriarch's destination as an "inheritance," the author uses Old Testament land-terminology but points to the eschatological focus of Abraham's faith. The author deduces from the phrase "the land that I will show thee" in Genesis 12:1 that Abraham acted on trust, not knowing where he was going. Although the promise of land was repeated to Abraham, he never saw its fulfillment, just as Israel did not inherit the promised rest—it was the *Promised* Land, not the *possessed* land.

The nomadic existence of Abraham, Isaac and Jacob, despite the repeated promise of land they had been given, highlights the tension between promise and earthly fulfillment. Abraham endured the unfulfilled promise, as symbolized by the impermanence of living in tents ("tabernacles" in the KJV) because he looked forward to living in a permanent city.

A textual problem occurs in Hebrews 11:11. The *King James Version* states that Sarah is the subject of the action: "Through faith also Sarah herself received strength to conceive seed, and was delivered of a child when she was past age, because she judged him faithful who had promised." However, other translations, such as *The New Revised Standard Version*, indicate that Abraham is the subject, adding the phrase "and Sarah herself was barren." That Abraham is the subject of this passage can be seen in the following:

- The wording of verses 11 and 12 seem to indicate that Abraham is the natural subject; "too old" and "as good as dead" are parallel descriptions for the same person.
- The "power of procreation" refers to the function of the male in begetting, rather than to that of the woman in conceiving.
- Sarah laughed because of unbelief at the thought of conceiving, though she later laughed with joy at Isaac's birth. Abraham also laughed at the idea of having a child at his age, but Genesis 15:6 specifically says that Abraham believed God's promise.

The author finds evidence for the eschatological nature of Abraham's faith in the patriarch's purchasing the cave of Machpelah to bury Sarah. The actions of the patriarch are a continuing witness to the existence of a final homeland for the Israelites that is not equated with Canaan as their temporary home, or with Mesopotamia, which was their original homeland. What they longed for, as the author states in verse 16, is a better country, with "better" referring to what is heavenly in origin and therefore lasting. This better country corresponds to the city with foundations. Faith in the promises of God, expressed in the patriarchs' confession, met with God's confession of them, and He was "not ashamed to be called their God." To be ashamed of someone means to not recognize them; the opposite means to openly acknowledge them. By allowing Himself to be called the God of Abraham, Isaac and Jacob, God acknowledges the faith of the fathers, a faith that is well founded, by preparing a city for them.

As with the first example of Abel's persevering faith in verse 4, a sacrifice is involved. The story of Abraham's readiness to sacrifice his son is one that has been widely

THE FAITH OF THE PATRIARCHS

commented on, but here the author is interested only in the testing of Abraham's faith. God's command to Abraham to sacrifice his only son was not only offensive to his paternal love but also attacked the very promise that Abraham had been given that he would be the father of a great nation. Isaac, not Ishmael, was to be the bearer of these promises. The writer sees in Abraham's submission a perfect demonstration of faith as trusting obedience. The patriarch places his faith in the promise itself and expresses it through his own assurance to his servants that he and the boy would return.

In Hebrews 11:19, the author shows how Abraham's faith was rewarded through the rescue of Isaac from virtual death. This was a symbolic foreshadowing of the future resurrection of Jesus Christ, to which Abraham could look in hope. God the Father readily surrendered His only Son, and then rescued Him from death.

The faith of Isaac, Jacob and Joseph illustrate this same hope as enunciated in verse 13: they "died in faith." By blessing their heirs when mentioning a future deliverance, they showed unwavering trust in God's promises, even though these promises ran contrary to human expectation. Jacob was also accepted as God's choice as the future bearer of the promise.

Jacob's blessing of Joseph's sons—even though they were born in Egypt and not the Promised Land—means that they were included among his own sons as bearers of blessing. The emphasis lies on "when dying" and on the posture of the patriarch. In death, Jacob adored God as the author of blessings and promises, and the staff in His hands marked him as a pilgrim on the move to the heavenly homeland.

The Faith of Moses and the Exodus Generation

> By faith Moses, when he was born, was hid three months of his parents, because they saw he was a proper child; and they were not afraid of the king's commandment. By faith Moses, when he was come to years, refused to be called the son of Pharaoh's daughter; choosing rather to suffer affliction with the people of God, than to enjoy the pleasures of sin for a season; esteeming the reproach of Christ greater riches than the treasures in Egypt: for he had respect unto the recompence of the reward. By faith he forsook Egypt, not fearing the wrath of the king: for he endured, as seeing him who is invisible. Through faith he kept the Passover, and the sprinkling of blood, lest he that destroyed the firstborn should touch them. By faith they passed through the Red sea as by dry land: which the Egyptians assaying to do were drowned. By faith the walls of Jericho fell down, after they were compassed about seven days. By faith the harlot Rahab perished not with them that believed not, when she had received the spies with peace.
> —Hebrews 11:23-31

The author of Hebrews now clearly identifies faith with perseverance in the face of opposition and suffering. Faith motivated Moses' parents to ignore Pharaoh's edict that all male infants be killed; they trusted God to preserve their child for his future task. Faith in divine provision removes fear. The author notes that the first example of Moses' own faith was illustrated through his rejection of earthly security, making him a companion of Abraham. Instead of enjoying princely luxury and prestige, Moses chose to identify with his own people, even though this meant sharing their ill treatment rather than enjoying "the pleasures of sin for a season."

THE FAITH OF THE PATRIARCHS

In choosing suffering over fleeting pleasures, the author assumes that Moses was fully aware of both his call to lead Israel and his call toward a lasting reward. Moses typifies the life of faith that involves suffering for Jesus Christ. By choosing suffering over prestige, he serves as a model of faith for those who are called to leave earthly security and bear abuse for Christ. Moses is the antithesis of the apostate who denies membership in God's people by denying Christ and refusing to suffer for him.

Moses left Egypt twice: once to escape punishment for murder, and a second time to participate in the Exodus. Although his first flight was motivated by fear for his personal safety, latter tradition sees it as exemplifying his confidence and endurance. Moses heard God's voice from the burning bush and spoke face to face with God without actually seeing God's face. He trusted God to lead the people out of slavery and perceived the truth of an invisible but eternal world in contrast to the attractiveness of any temporary, earthly home. The writer shows special interest in the life-giving power of the blood, so he focuses attention on the application of the blood, not on the Passover meal.

The author's inclusion of Rahab the harlot is an unlikely candidate as an example of faith. She and Sarah are the only women in this catalogue, but she seems to have a special interest for early Christians. In harboring the Israelites who were sent out by Joshua to spy out Jericho, she aligned herself with the wandering people of God and expressed her faith in God's ability to give them the Promised Land. Her faith initially put her life at risk, but ultimately led to her rescue from the fate suffered by those in Jericho (as well as future unbelievers).

The Faith of Subsequent Generations

> And what shall I more say? For the time would fail me to tell of Gedeon, and of Barak, and of Samson, and of Jephthae: of David also, and Samuel, and of the prophets: Who through faith subdued kingdoms, wrought righteousness, obtained promises, stopped the mouths of lions, quenched the violence of fire, escaped the edge of the sword, out of weakness were made strong, waxed valiant in fight, turned to flight the armies of the aliens. Women received their dead raised to life again: and others were tortured, not accepting deliverance; that they might obtain a better resurrection: And others had trial of cruel mockings and scourgings, yea, moreover of bonds and imprisonment: They were stoned, they were sawn asunder, were tempted, were slain with the sword: they wandered about in sheepskins and goatskins; being destitute, afflicted, tormented; (of whom the world was not worthy:) they wandered in deserts, and in mountains, and in dens and caves of the earth. And these all, having obtained a good report through faith, received not the promise: God having provided some better things for us, that they without us should not be made perfect.
> —Hebrews 11:32-40

In this final passage, the writer gives a sampling of six figures from the period of the judges and the early monarchy (Barak, Gideon, Jephithah, Samson, Samuel and David) without comment. God called Barak through the prophetess Deborah to defeat a league of Canaanites, while Gideon rescued Israel from the Midianites with a small force of 300 men. Jephthah led the eastern tribes against the Ammonites, and Samson's proverbial strength and cunning led to victories over the Philistines. David received the promise of an eternal throne, fulfilled in Christ. His psalms bear testimony to his deep faith in God. The author lists

THE FAITH OF THE PATRIARCHS

Samuel, the last charismatic judge, possibly after David in order to associate him with the prophets.

It was primarily Joshua, the judges, David and Solomon who "through faith subdued kingdoms" by capturing Canaan and extending Israel's borders. Samuel, David and Solomon "wrought righteousness" by administering justice. "Obtained promises" refers to military victories, such as those promised to Barak, Gideon, Samson and David, and to the gift of wealth promised to Solomon. David "escaped the edge of the sword" by overcoming Goliath, Saul and Absalom, and prophets such as Elijah, Elisha and Jeremiah escaped the murderous plots of rulers.

God empowered the weak like Gideon, who gained victory with a small army. He restored Samson's strength for one last triumph. David defeated Goliath with only a sling and a stone. Judith and Esther were women who led the Israelites to victory. Elijah and Elisha vindicated the faith of weak and defenseless women, like the widow at Zarepath and the Shunammite woman, by raising their sons from the dead. Like Abraham, they trusted God to create life where there was only death.

The author's reference to resurrection in 11:35 provides the link to the story of the martyrs' faith. They endured appalling suffering, placing their hope in a better resurrection than the restoration of an earthly, normal life. Jeremiah was the type of suffering prophet who endured insults, beatings and confinement. Elijah and Elisha, wearing only sheepskins and goatskins, were marked as itinerant prophets, separate from city life and its comforts. Even while escaping death, the prophets suffered extreme privation. One hundred prophets took refuge from Queen Jezebel in caves; Elijah had to flee to the desert.

Destitute and tormented, the prophets were the forerunners of later martyrs who fled to remote areas to escape persecution. Later in Jewish history, Judas Maccabeus and his companions lived like wild animals in the mountains. Such martyrs, rejected by society, belong to a better world. Like Abraham and Moses, they spurned this life for something better and more enduring. That is why God commends their faith in the form of scriptural attestation.

Application

These martyrs received various promises, but only partial fulfillment of those promises in their lifetime. This was not due to any fault on their part, but was ordained by divine providence. God's ultimate promise was fulfilled in Jesus Christ, through whom believers have now received something better.

The author implies that past believers who once lived in hope of perfection without receiving it now experience it in glory. His argument in verse 40 does not aim at exclusion but inclusion. Those who look forward to the realization of God's promises and those who can now look back to their partial fulfillment are finally united in the one faith.

In worship, Christians are already part of the heavenly city and united with the spirits of the righteous made perfect. Nevertheless, until they are perfected with Jesus Christ in glory, they must emulate the enduring faith of past witnesses who kept their faith focused and fixed their gaze on future realities.

HEBREWS XII

RUN WITH DISCIPLINE THE COURSE SET BY JESUS

God Disciplines His Children

> Wherefore seeing we also are compassed about with so great a cloud of witnesses, let us lay aside every weight, and the sin which doth so easily beset us, and let us run with patience the race that is set before us, looking unto Jesus the author and finisher of our faith; who for the joy that was set before him endured the cross, despising the shame, and is set down at the right hand of the throne of God. For consider him that endured such contradiction of sinners against himself, let ye be wearied and faint in your minds. Ye have not yet resisted unto blood, striving against sin. And ye have forgotten the exhortation which speaketh unto you as unto children, My son, despise not thou the chastening of the Lord, nor faint when thou art rebuked of him: For whom the Lord loveth he chasteneth, and scourgeth every son whom he receiveth. If ye endure chastening, God dealeth with you as with sons; for what son is he whom the father chasteneth not? But if ye be without chastisement, whereof all are partakers, then are ye bastards, and not sons. Furthermore we have had

fathers of our flesh which corrected us, and we gave them reverence: shall we not much rather be in subjection unto the Father of spirits, and live? For they verily for a few days chastened us after their own pleasure; but he for our profit, that we might be partakers of his holiness. Now no chastening for the present seemeth to be joyous, but grievous: nevertheless afterward it yieldeth the peaceable fruit of righteousness unto them which are exercised thereby.
—Hebrews 12:1-11

THE AUTHOR'S USE of athletic imagery in verses 1-4 suggests that the "cloud of witnesses" surround Christian athletes like spectators in an arena. The phrase "the race that is set before us" is a fixed phrase in classical and Hellenistic Greek and is used as an athletic metaphor to denote the concerted effort required in attaining a goal. Runners do not determine the course or the condition of the race.

The author keeps to his main theme: the need for stamina to endure the rigors of the contest. The athlete must strip off excess weight that would impede his progress, which might be the desire for earthly security and social acceptance. The one encumbrance that must be shed is the sin that clings so closely, which is any besetting sin that might cause the runner to fall. On the other hand, it could be something that easily distracts his attention from achieving the goal.

Christians look to Jesus Christ as their prime source of encouragement. He is the one on whom their faith depends from start to finish. He remains the faithful and obedient Son from beginning to the end. The author also notes that Jesus endured suffering with the prospect of future joy. The cross, as a symbol of shame, contrasts with the honor represented by enthronement at God's right hand. In a similar way, Moses also endured abuse by looking forward to a reward.

RUN WITH DISCIPLINE THE COURSE SET BY JESUS

By inference, the author states that the persecutions the Christians are suffering can be made lighter by the joyful prospect of the future glory that awaits them as guaranteed by the glorified Son. Jesus Christ is the prime example of enduring hostility in pursuit of a set goal. Those who attacked Him during His impassioned public ministry were sinners whose hostility was against themselves, which suggests that sin leads to self-injury. Believers who consider Christ by fixing their attention on His example will not grow weary in running the race that is set before them when they meet with opposition. The race involves antagonists who will stand in their path and with whom they must come to grips like a boxer or wrestler. The tone of verses 4-5 is exemplified in the phrase "to the point of shedding blood" ("ye have not yet resisted unto blood" in the KJV), implying the readers have not yet engaged in serious combat of the sort that produces blood in a wrestling or boxing match.

"Discipline" ("chastening" in the KJV) and "child" are the key words in the author's theme in verses 7-11. The opening sentence could be read as a statement or as a command. Not all human suffering is indicative of divine discipline; however, it is through trials endured as confessors of Jesus Christ that the readers are to recognize the parental love of God at work and confirmation of their status as God's children. Greater attention is lavished on legitimate children, in contrast to illegitimate children, in view of their status as heirs. Thus, suffering is a trait of being God's children and not an extraordinary experience.

In verses 9-11, the author contrasts earthly and divine discipline to show the gracious purpose of the latter. Collective wisdom teaches that discipline, administered appropriately by human parents, leads to respect. That God is Lord over angelic beings and the spirits of the dead is probably best understood in the anthropological sense.

Earthly fathers pass on physical life, but God is the creator of people as spirit-beings who will live eternally, even if their suffering leads to physical death.

Although God's children live the better life now and in the future by virtue of Jesus Christ's victory over the power of death, the promise of life to which the author refers in Hebrews 12:9 is not christological-based. Discipline from God is always good because it is based on a true assessment of needs, and is beneficial in that it promotes sound wisdom. It ensures that a person receives a share in God's holiness. Suffering is thus a divine means of preserving Christians in their status as God's special children.

The author depicts the testing that suffering provides in verse 11 as athletic training, which rounds off the image he began in verses 1-4. Enduring discipline is comparable to undergoing strenuous exercises, but the outcome makes all the pain worthwhile.

Remove All That Hinders Progress

> Wherefore lift up the hands which hang down, and the feeble knees; and make straight paths for your feet, lest that which is lame be turned out of the way; but let it rather be healed. Follow peace with all men, and holiness, without which no man shall see the Lord: Looking diligently lest any man fail of the grace of God; lest any root of bitterness springing up trouble you, and thereby many be defiled; lest there be any fornicator, or profane person, as Esau, who for one morsel of meat sold his birthright. For ye know how that afterward, when he would have inherited the blessing, he was rejected: for he found no place of repentance, though he sought it carefully with tears.
> —Hebrews 12:12-17

RUN WITH DISCIPLINE THE COURSE SET BY JESUS

The author states that the strong in faith are to make straight paths for the feet of those who are "lame," or weak in faith. Those wavering through exhaustion are to be strengthened and redirected to the goal so that they do not fall by the wayside. "Healing" denotes the present renewal of spiritual energies rather than the outcome of reaching the goal.

The fruit of divine discipline is peace, and it accompanies those who follow wisdom's path. The pursuit of peace means preserving a gift that comes from the God of peace. Communal harmony and solidarity in the face of suffering can be ensured only as the church lives in the wholeness that God works through Jesus Christ.

The sanctity that flows from the sacrifice of Jesus Christ and His cleansing blood is to be expressed in a life of corporate holiness. Holiness is necessary for believers to see the face of God, and it is also a reminder of His cultic setting. Purification by the blood of Jesus Christ creates the state of holiness that allows believers access into God's holy presence.

"The root of bitterness" is a stubborn turning away from God to idolatry. A noxious root will destroy all other roots if it is allowed to grow. Apostasy must be nipped in the bud before it disrupts the whole community.

The author cites Esau as an example of a godless or "profane person" because he behaved in an irreligious manner in selling a birthright that included a divine blessing. He chose monetary gratification through something profane, despising a holy gift with long-term effects. In verse 17, the author assumes an understanding of divine blessing and curse as performative words that, once spoken, cannot be revoked. When Esau wanted to reclaim the blessing he was refused, because the pronouncement was already made. The fact that Esau did not have a chance to repent means that he could not reverse the effects of his actions. The finality of apostasy makes repentance impossible.

Share in the New, Heavenly Worship

> For ye are not come unto the mount that might be touched, and that burned with fire, nor unto blackness, and darkness, and tempest, and the sound of a trumpet, and the voice of words; which voice they that heard entreated that the word should not be spoken to them any more: (For they could not endure that which was commanded, and if so much as a beast touch the mountain, it shall be stoned, or thrust through with a dart: And so terrible was the sight, that Moses said, I exceedingly fear and quake:) But ye are come unto mount Zion, and unto the city of the living God, the heavenly Jerusalem, and to an innumerable company of angels, to the general assembly and church of the firstborn, which are written in heaven, and to God the Judge of all, and to the spirits of just men made perfect, and to Jesus the mediator of the new covenant, and to the blood of sprinkling, that speaketh better things than that of Abel.
> —Hebrews 12:18-24

By using his favored expression for drawing near to God in worship, the writer recalls Israel's experience of God's holy presence at Mount Sinai: "That [which] might be touched" may mean the mountain itself. The mountain's tangibility marked it as belonging to the earthly realm in contrast to the heavenly Mount Zion.

The mysterious and terrifying sights (fire, darkness and gloom) and sounds (tempest, trumpet blast and heavenly voice) that surrounded the Israelites' experience at Mount Sinai marked the holy God as unapproachable. The writer of Hebrews closely associates the people's fear at this epiphany with the voice that uttered the interdict against touching

RUN WITH DISCIPLINE THE COURSE SET BY JESUS

the holy mountain; thus the people's plea that all further communications from God be directed through Moses (see Exodus 19:16-23; 20:18-19). On the other hand, Moses expressed extreme fear at the entire manifestation of divine majesty (see Deuteronomy 9:19).

For the author, the objective realities to which Christians have come under the new covenant, where fear is replaced with festivity, is made clear by the subjective experience of Israel. The "city of the living God" is the heavenly sanctuary or temple, and its inhabitants are the myriad angels. They attended the theophany at Mount Sinai and now surround God's heavenly throne. They form a festal gathering. In coming to the heavenly city/sanctuary in worship, Christians are united with angelic hosts.

The author suggests that Christians belong to an assembly of God's elect in which earthly praise is joined to heavenly. The divine judge is the vindicator of the righteous who lived by faith. All who were cleansed by Jesus Christ's sacrifice are already perfected in this life, but those who have died in the faith are perfected in the same sense as Christ—they are now glorified with Him.

This gathering of the saints is founded on Jesus Christ and His sacrifice. The old covenant at Mount Sinai was mediated through a fear-filled Moses and inaugurated with animal sacrifice. Jesus Christ mediates the new covenant through His self-sacrifice. Believers come to God through Jesus Christ's atoning sacrifice in the past, but they also come to Him as the living guarantor of a better covenant in the present, because He intercedes for the saints at God's right hand.

Old Testament ritual required the application of animal blood, but a better cleansing is effected by Jesus Christ's blood. The blood of Jesus continues to have cleansing power for those who enter the heavenly sanctuary. The blood of Abel, one of those who lived by faith, once cried out for vengeance. Christ's blood continues to speak, but with a better word; its message is one of effective cleansing from sin. This word is not addressed to God, but the word comes from God.

Final Warning: Do Not Reject God's Warnings

> See that ye refuse not him that speaketh. For if they escaped not who refused him that spake on earth, much more shall not we escape, if we turn away from him that speaketh from heaven: Whose voice then shook the earth; but now he hath promised, saying, yet once more I shake not the earth only, but also heaven. And this word, yet once more, signifieth the removing of those things that are shaken, as of things that are made, that those things which cannot be shaken may remain. Wherefore we receiving a kingdom which cannot be moved, let us have grace, whereby we may serve God acceptably with reverence and godly fear: For our God is a consuming fire.
> —Hebrews 12:25-29

The author states that God is now speaking clearly and powerfully, in comparison with when He spoke Mount Sinai, so refusal to listen to His voice is even more reprehensible. The voice that now comes from the heavenly Zion speaks an eternal message, so escape from the divine punishment for rejecting God's eschatological message in the new covenant is now even less possible. It is God, not Moses, who issues the warning, and it is clear that the writer is referring to the apocalyptic notion of a final shaking of the universe. There will be a shaking of the created universe, of earth and sky, on the Day of Judgment. The final removal of the created order points to the permanent durability of the heavenly order. The transitory must give way to the eternal.

RUN WITH DISCIPLINE THE COURSE SET BY JESUS

God's saints will posses the kingdom forever. The idea that the readers are receiving this kingdom implies that the shaking spoken of in Haggai 2:6 ("For thus saith the LORD of hosts; yet once, it is a little while, and I will shake the heavens, and the earth, and the sea, and the dry land") started with the work of Christ and will climax in His exaltation. How the reader responds to God's final revelation will indicate whether or not he or she is part of God's kingdom. The wrong response is rejection; the only fitting response is to give thanks. Through their High Priest's sacrifice and the power of His cleansing blood, the faithful can serve the living God with their sacrifice of praise. The sacrifice of praise and confession is acceptable worship because it is offered in faith. It includes a life of good works that is pleasing to God.

Reverence and awe is appropriate in the presence of the holy God who is a consuming fire. A fiery judgment will destroy anything impure and unholy.

HEBREWS XIII

THE OFFERING OF BROTHERLY LOVE

Virtues to Be Exhibited in the Persecuted Community

Let brotherly love continue. Be not forgetful to entertain strangers: for thereby some have entertained angels unawares. Remember them that are in bonds, as bound with them; and them which suffer adversity, as being yourselves also in the body. Marriage is honourable in all, and the bed undefiled: but whoremongers and adulterers God will judge. Let your conversation be without covetousness; and be content with such things as ye have: for he hath said, I will never leave thee, nor forsake thee. So that we may boldly say, The Lord is my helper, and I will not fear what man shall do unto me.
—Hebrews 13:1-6

THIS SECTION CONTAINS four pairs of commands, each addressing a related issue:

1. Mutual love and hospitality
2. Care for the imprisoned and tortured

3. Respect for marriage and avoidance of adultery
4. Rejection of greed and pursuit of contentment

Virtues like love, hospitality, compassion, chastity and contentment are expected of any Christian group. These verses echo early catechetic instruction, but the context suggests a pointed application: in addition to a life of holiness, it is vital for a community under threat of persecution to exhibit specific virtues. Love sets Christians apart from the world and gives them cohesion as a group to stand united against its attacks. A good record in the past is no guarantee that love, like faith and hope, will not grow cold. Hospitality is one such concrete expression of love within the Christian family. Times of persecution increase the need for believers to have homes in which they can take temporary refuge,

The author's exhortation for the readers to remember those in prison includes sympathetic identification that finds expression in communal prayer on their behalf. Solidarity also means identifying with those being tortured, suffering physical abuse, or verbal maligning. The marriage bed must also be undefiled, because marriage is a sacrosanct ordering of life and a prime area in which to maintain cultic cleanness. A clean record in the area of sexuality will help the community blunt the attacks of outsiders. God's judgment falls on the sexually impure.

The readers were not dismayed by past loss but by threats of renewed social hostility that could make them anxious about their homes and other properties, so the writer reminds them that to value temporal things more than the coming kingdom is not worthy of those who are destined to inherit lasting possessions. Practical expressions of love must always complement the confession of faith.

THE OFFERING OF BROTHERLY LOVE

Life Within the Worshiping Community

> Remember them which have the rule over you, who have spoken unto you the word of God: whose faith follow, considering the end of their conversation. Jesus Christ the same yesterday, and today, and forever. Be not carried about with divers and strange doctrines. For it is a good thing that the heart be established with grace; not with meats, which have not profited them that have been occupied therein. We have an altar, whereof they have no right to eat which serve the tabernacle. For the bodies of those beasts, whose blood is brought into the sanctuary by the high priest for sin, are burned without the camp. Wherefore Jesus also, that he might sanctify the people with his own blood, suffered without the gate. Let us go forth therefore unto him without the camp, bearing his reproach. For here have we no continuing city, but we seek one to come. By him therefore let us offer the sacrifice of praise to God continually, that is, the fruit of our lips giving thanks to his name. But to do good and to communicate forget not: for with such sacrifices God is well pleased. Obey them that have the rule over you, and submit yourselves: for they watch for your souls, as they that must give account, that they may do it with joy, and not with grief: for that is unprofitable for you. Pray for us: for we trust we have a good conscience, in all things willing to live honestly. But I beseech you the rather to do this, that I may be restored to you the sooner.
>
> —Hebrews 13:7-19

The author's instruction to the community to remember past leaders who spoke God's Word implies more than recalling the community's founders. When God remembers His covenant or His people, He reenacts His promises and saving works. When people remember God's promises and His acts of deliverance, they celebrate the past as present reality. Contemplation of past leaders is a reminder of grace and thus produces praise to God. The believer's consideration of past leaders who were faithful should lead to fixing his or her eyes upon Jesus Christ as the ultimate leader and example of faithful endurance.

To confess Jesus Christ is to celebrate His constant and unchanging presence. Confession of praise to the unchanging intercessor is not to be exchanged for false teaching.

The connection between eating and sacrifice in verses 9-11 and the call to follow Jesus Christ outside the city gate in verses 12-14 may hint at a more-than-symbolic meaning for foods. It is possible that some in the community found social acceptance and security in continued participation in other cultic meals. The author calls for the readers to break with earthly securities by reminding them that their security lies in the grace of God. Taking part in non-Christian cultic meals constitutes a threat to their existence, denies God's grace, and indicates a departure from the teaching of past leaders.

The altar stands for Christ's sacrificial death, and those who serve at the earthly altar have no right to partake in His sacrifice. His perfect sacrifice continues to mediate grace in the form of perfect cleansing from sin. The sacrificial system of the old covenant could not do this.

By speaking of the bodies of animals, and by recalling the action of the high priest in applying the blood, the author hints at the action of the heavenly High Priest in presenting His life-giving blood in the heavenly sanctuary. Christians who are sanctified by Jesus Christ's blood belong with Him outside of the earthly tabernacle and its sacrifices. To "go out" thus means to separate from others because of being made holy.

THE OFFERING OF BROTHERLY LOVE

Those who seek God must now come to Jesus, who was rejected inside the city. The writer here refers to the distinction between sacred and profane places and to Christ's suffering in history. He also gives a probable social setting for a community that is bearing abuse for Christ.

In the thanksgiving psalms, praise often appears as a declaratory confession of God's name and gracious deeds. God's promises are all fulfilled through Jesus Christ, who enables people to approach the divine throne in worship. That praise and thanksgiving are to be matched by ethical actions is suggested by Psalm 50:23 ("Who so offereth praise glorifieth me: and to him that ordereth his conversation aright will I show the salvation of God"), but the author drew a connection between confession, good deeds and worship earlier in the letter:

> Let us hold fast the profession of our faith without wavering; (for he is faithful that promised;) and let us consider one another to provoke unto love and to good works: Not forsaking the assembling of ourselves together, as the manner of some is; but exhorting one another: and so much the more, as ye see the day approaching.
> —Hebrews 10:23-25

Doing "good works" includes all acts of kindness for those in need and is performed as service to God.

The author states that the community's obedience and submission to their leaders is required in view of those leaders' function as spiritual guardians. The guides he refers to here are probably the successors of those whose remembrance the believers are exhorted to cherish in verse 7. The author has confidence in their present leaders as well as in their predecessors. These individuals could be leaders in the city church from whose fellowship and jurisdiction the community addressed in the letter were lured to withdraw. The leaders carried a heavy responsibility because they were accountable for the spiritual wellbeing of the people placed in their custody. The leaders' responsibility to serve others certainly means that they will one day give account to God for their ministry. The community's ready obedience will make their leaders' task joyful, but grudging compliance will make them sigh or grumble.

There would have definitely been a propensity throughout the churches at the time for guests who preached new and esoteric doctrines to be regarded as interesting celebrities, especially when compared to the rather monotonous local leaders who never taught anything new but were comfortable with the apostolic traditional conservative line. However, it was the local leaders, not the purveyors of bizarre teachings, who had genuine concern for the welfare of the church and knowledge of their accountability to God in this regard. Opposition to leaders will register present and eternal loss. Faithfulness to the truth, attested by past leaders and contained in the confession to Jesus Christ, means rejection of error.

A Personal Conclusion

> Now the God of peace, that brought again from the dead our Lord Jesus, that great shepherd of the sheep, through the blood of the everlasting covenant, make you perfect in every good work to do his will, working in you that which is wellpleasing in his sight, through Jesus Christ; to whom be glory for ever and ever. Amen. And I beseech you, brethren, suffer the word of exhortation: for I have written a letter unto you in few words. Know ye that our brother Timothy is set at liberty; with whom, if he come shortly, I will see you. Salute all them that have the rule

THE OFFERING OF BROTHERLY LOVE

over you, and all the saints. They of Italy salute you. Grace be with you all. Amen.

—Hebrews 13:20-25

"The God of peace" appears to be a fixed liturgical phrase; it also occurs in concluding blessings and prayers in Paul's letters. In the above prayer, the writer anticipates the end of the worship assembly in which the letter is being read. The word "peace" refers to the wholeness of salvation. The "word of exhortation" refers to the entire preceding epistle. In Acts 13:15, where the rulers of the synagogue at Pisidian Antioch sent a message to Paul and Barnabas to appeal to them to pass on any "word of exhortation" that they had for the assembled company, the phrase signifies a homily; thus, it is a suitable description for this letter, which is a written homily with personal remarks. Could a document of this length be written in a "few words"? If we regard it as a letter, it is not as long as Romans or 1 or 2 Corinthians.

The author concludes his letter by sounding a call to worship as an expression of confident faith. He begins his concluding lines with prayer and ends with a blessing. The prayer recalls the central message of the letter, reminding the readers that they are a new covenant people, sanctified by the blood of Jesus Christ. Christ is their new leader in worship. Certainly, Timothy refers to Paul's friend of that name, though we do not have any other account of his imprisonment. The author notes that he has been "set free" ("set at liberty" in the KJV); he might mention this because the place of Timothy's imprisonment, while some distance from the author's residence, is closer to him than to his readers. He has information of Timothy's discharge in advance of his readers, and he wants them to know that if Timothy arrives soon, the two of them will come to visit the church together. Earlier the author exhorted them to obey their leaders, and now he requests that they express his compliments to them and to the entire fellowship of believers. This would include members of other houses of worship than their own in the citywide fellowship to which they belonged.

These last verses are proof of the writer's pastoral heart. Concerned for the integrity of the readers' faith and practice, for their own unity, and for continued fellowship with him, he could have issued harsh warnings and threats of divine punishment. However, his word of exhortation becomes a word of comfort. The benediction is identical with that of Titus 3:15.

In conclusion, the author's main purpose in writing this letter to the Hebrews is to show that those who are Christians are so because of a high caliber of certain acts of God that occurred previously at a definite time. These acts of God released a dynamic power that does not allow Christians to rest at any time short of the divine rest, which, though difficult to achieve, is to be the goal in this life. God calls people to faith anew so that they can lead the saints to new endeavors in the cause of Jesus Christ. The faith that was delivered once and for all to the saints is not something that can be caught and controlled. Abraham did not know where he might be led, but his faith in the unchanging God prepared him to do the bidding of God.

There are diverse enticements in this world that make the author's message an essential and salutary one for us at this time of the end. We may be putting ourselves in great danger by following certain religious attitudes or activities for the simple reason that they were good enough for our fathers and grandfathers. All new movements of the Spirit of God tend to become stereotyped in following generations. What we have heard with our ears and from our fathers

THE OFFERING OF BROTHERLY LOVE

may turn out to be a tenacious custom that encroaches on the loyalty that ought to be accorded the living and lively word of God Almighty.

As Christians, there is much that is waiting for us to possess in the name of Jesus Christ, but there is no way we can take possession of those things without an onward-looking faith. This is what the author of Hebrews urges upon his readers. The first readers lived at a time when the old order was breaking up, and the author knew that attachment to the unchanging and forward-moving Jesus Christ could lift them and enable them to face a new order with confidence and power.

Let us give thanks to God Almighty for the unshakable kingdom we have inherited, which will endure from everlasting to everlasting when all other things that are human will disappear in a twinkle of an eye.

BIBLIOGRAPHY

WORKS CITED

Bruce, F. F. *The Epistle to the Hebrews*. NICNT. Grand Rapids, MI: Eerdmans, 1990.

Fjordbak, Everitt M. *An Exposition and Commentary on the Epistle to the Hebrews*. Dallas, TX: Wisdom House Publishers, 1983.

Hagner, Donald A. *Encountering the Book of Hebrews*, Grand Rapids, MI: Baker Academic, 2002.

Pfitzner, Victor C. *Abingdon New Testament Commentaries: Hebrews*. Nashville, TN: Abingdon Press, 1997.

Westcott, Brooke F. *The Epistle to the Hebrews*. Grand Rapids, MI: Eerdmans Publishing Company, 1965.

Commentary on Hebrews, *www.blueletterbible.org*, accessed November 4, 2004.

TO CONTACT THE AUTHOR PLEASE WRITE TO

Samson Adewole Adedokun

PO Box 380610 Duncanville, TX 75138-0610 USA

Or please visit the companion Web site for this book at
www.thecompassionategod.com
for additional resources.

Please let me know if The Compassionate God has had an effect in your life or in the lives of your loved ones.

To order additional copies of this book call:
1-877-421-READ (7323)
or please visit our Web site at
www.WinePressbooks.com

If you enjoyed this quality custom-published book,
drop by our Web site for more books and information.

www.winepressgroup.com
"Your partner in custom publishing."

ALSO AVAILABLE IN E-BOOK FORMAT.

CPSIA information can be obtained at www.ICGtesting.com
Printed in the USA
LVOW041022080312